THE SIX WEEKS TO *Sexy* ABS MEAL PLAN

THE SECRET TO LOSING THOSE LAST SIX POUNDS:
A PLANT-BASED NUTRITION PROGRAM AND RECIPES

ELLA MAGERS
FOUNDER OF SEXY FIT VEGAN

PAGE STREET
PUBLISHING CO.

First published in 2015 by

Page Street Publishing Co.

27 Congress Street, Suite 103

Salem, MA 01970

www.pagestreetpublishing.com

Distributed by Macmillan, sales in Canada by The Canadian Manda Group.

18   17   16   15   1 2 3 4 5

ISBN-13: 9781624141430

ISBN-10: 1624141439

Library of Congress Control Number: 2015939048

Cover and book design by Page Street Publishing Co.

Photography by Grace Dickinson, Michael Reh and Anthony Gaston

Printed and bound in China

Page Street is proud to be a member of 1% for the Planet. Members donate one percent of their sales to one or more of the over 1,500 environmental and sustainability charities across the globe who participate in this program.

To my mom and dad, who have always
given me the unconditional love, freedom and
support I've needed to simply be me.

Contents

FOREWORD

I knew I'd discovered someone special when I first met Ella at the 2014 Seed Food and Wine Festival in Miami. I said to myself, "Here is a woman who practices what she preaches and embodies her beliefs." I am thrilled that she has decided to share her fit vegan lifestyle with the rest of us.

Whether you want to contour your booty, sculpt your midsection, fit into your favorite jeans again or know what it feels like to eat clean and green, following Ella's plan will put you on track. She lays out a clear, easy-to-follow program that is also practical and efficient. This book covers your bases, answers your questions and addresses your concerns. Ella's Six Weeks to Sexy Abs Plan is do-able for anyone and everyone.

What does it mean for your body to leave meat, dairy and eggs behind, replacing them with whole foods, fresh fruits, vegetables, whole grains, legumes, nuts and seeds? The changes in your outward physical appearance are obvious, and the FEELING GOOD from the inside out, on a cellular level, are life changing. Highly functioning organs make our bodies run smoothly, keep us healthy and clear-minded, and prevent, treat and cure disease while slowing the aging process. What seem like miracles aren't actually miracles because they come to fruition based on our own food choices. Once we have the knowledge, we have the power to change our lives, and Ella brings us the information we need in this book.

I am a 15-year NBA veteran and 8-year vegan. Adopting a plant-based diet helped me drop unwanted pounds, boost my libido and gain a feeling of health and well-being. Embrace your power with Ella and the Six Weeks to Sexy Abs Plan by your side and get ready to celebrate the results!

—John Salley, Wellness Advocate, NBA Champion & TV Host

INTRODUCTION

Six Weeks to Sexy Abs: What It's All About

Do you find yourself feeling frustrated and asking, "Why can't I drop these last few pounds?" You may exercise consistently and think you "eat healthy," yet those last few nagging pounds of body fat just won't seem to budge. *The Six Weeks to Sexy Abs Meal Plan* is here to the rescue!

Becoming fit and healthy from the inside out, dropping those last few annoying pounds and feeling sexy from head to toe—that's what the Six Weeks to Sexy Abs Plan is all about. You're certainly not alone in your quest to fit into those skinny jeans that are just a bit too skinny, if you know what I mean. With this program, in just 42 days you could be ready to wear those jeans with confidence and a big smile.

This is NOT just another fad diet. It's time to be done with popular diets you've been brainwashed into thinking are viable solutions. Diets that have the dreaded "yo-yo" effect are unsustainable, leave you feeling like crap and have negative long-term effects on your health. *The Six Weeks to Sexy Abs Meal Plan* does none of that! This program is designed to jumpstart you into a lifestyle that will sculpt a strong, lean body for a lifetime! As if that wasn't enough, with this plan you also get the bonus benefit of contributing to a better world by reducing your environmental footprint and saving the lives of animals. Think of Six Weeks to Sexy Abs as a fresh start to a new body and healthy way of life.

Before I continue, let me introduce myself. I'm Ella Magers and I developed the Six Weeks to Sexy Abs Plan based on both my own experiences and the 12 years of experience I have working with clients who are ready to change their bodies and lives.

In order to understand how the Six Weeks to Sexy Abs Plan came to be, it would be helpful for you to have some background information. Here's a glimpse of how it all transpired.

If you asked me, "Ella, what do you care most deeply about in this world? What is your greatest passion?" My answer would be: "Ending animal cruelty, and motivating, educating and inspiring people to become fit, healthy and happy." In fact, if you asked me those very same questions when I was in grade school, my answers would be the same, only in the words of child, of course. Take a look!

It's fair to say that I've been devoted to motivating, educating and inspiring people to live in a way that is conscious and compassionate to animals, the environment AND themselves for 28 of my 35 years!

When it comes to fitness, I've been active in sports since I was five years old. I was a competitive swimmer, gymnast and volleyball player growing up. As an adult, I've been practicing Muay Thai and countless other types of workouts and activities for over 12 years. I've excelled athletically on a plant-based diet my whole life. I started long before most people even knew what "vegan" meant, so it was up to me to

Ella Magers
Health 7
8/30/91

What Do I Believe In

I believe that killing any kind of animal for any reason is wrong. If I could have it my way everybody would be a vegatarien like I am now. They wouldn't eat fish or chicken or anything that is alive. I believe that because we have got so many other things we can eat why should we have to kill something. Besides, what have they done to us?

Ella Magers
Health
9/9/90

Define Physical Fitness...

Physical fitness is being healthy. It is being in good condition. Eating healthy meals, exercising and feeling good abut yourself.

Why Is It Important to be Physically Fit...

It is important to be physically fit because you need to be strong and healthy. You will be able to achieve higher goals in life. You will feel better about yourself.

How Does a Person Know If Their Physically Fit...

A person knows if their physically fit if they are strong. Also, if they eat good food and feel good about who they are.

educate myself on nutrition and create my own meal plans. However, I've never been interested in spending much time in the kitchen, so not only did I develop expertise on healthy plant-based meals over the years, but also on quick and easy plant-based meals!

After college, I jumped right into the field of health and fitness. I eagerly became a trainer and coach, psyched to help people improve their lives. I soon discovered that in order for my clients to break their unhealthy habits, they needed a solid plan of action. My clients wanted a program that would work for a busy individual who needed a simple and efficient workout and nutrition plan to fit their packed schedule. I could relate to their plight! Spending the majority of my life discovering how to eat the healthiest diet possible with the least amount of time and effort began benefiting not only myself, but my clients as well. I was thrilled to have an outlet to share my tricks of the trade! I was living proof that you can be strong and fit on a plant-based diet and maintain a fun and exciting lifestyle at the same time.

Sexy Fit Vegan® was soon born in order to share with people all over the world how to eat and train for the lean, toned body they desire, feel great from the inside out and be sexy from head to toe. In 2007, I competed in the FAME World Championships, a bodybuilding and fitness competition, in order to show the world what a healthy vegan diet can do for your physique. I was proud to take first place in the bikini division, and second in the fitness and fitness model categories. I was also recognized by Bodybuilding.com, the most popular bodybuilding and fitness website in the world, being named Personal Trainer of the Month in September 2013. Additionally, I was honored to be named in *Shape* magazine's "Top 50 Hottest Trainers in America 2014."

The valuable recognition I received from FAME, Bodybuilding.com, *Shape* magazine, and other reputable companies was the catalyst for me to begin worldwide ventures to spread my message on how to live healthfully and compassionately. It was when I traveled to China to lead workshops for the Sheraton Macao's fitness month that I realized it was time to put my knowledge and experience into writing. I developed Six Weeks to Sexy Abs to provide that solid, practical plan of action you need to make significant progress in a short period of time by eating balanced and delicious meals every day.

There you have it, my story in a nutshell. You'll get to know me better through my narration as you read on, but I'm just as excited as you are to get to the Plan, so let's get started. I want to thank you for entrusting me to be your coach for the next six weeks. Let's do this!

CHAPTER 1

WHY THE PLAN Works

Now that you've gotten to know me a little better, I'm sure you're curious to find out what the Six Weeks to Sexy Abs Plan entails, so let's dive in! The majority of our focus in this book will be on diet. Why? It's simple. You can't outrun your fork. What I mean is, no matter how much you exercise or how hard you train, you'll never get the results you want unless you are eating the right foods. Ready for this? You have to jog over two miles (3.2 km) to burn off the empty calories in one, grab-size bag of potato chips... Ouch!

The Six Weeks to Sexy Abs Plan is here to guide you through six weeks of eating clean and green, without sacrificing the flavors and textures of foods you love. Take a minute to visualize yourself six weeks down the road, pounds lighter, feeling better than ever. How motivated will you be then? Especially when you love what you're eating and how it makes you feel!

Whether a plant-based diet is new to you or not, embrace the Six Weeks to Sexy Abs Plan as a life-changing challenge. **It's not about dieting; it's about eating according to your goals.** If losing those last few pounds of body fat is your goal, healthy plant-based eating is the path that will get you there and keep you there more effectively than a diet that includes animal products. The results make it well worth the discipline it takes to stick to the plan.

The Six Weeks to Sexy Abs Plan is designed to carefully guide you toward your goals with structure and support. Remember, you're creating permanent, positive changes in your body and health! You've already made the first huge step—caring enough to pick up this book and start reading! It's important to give yourself credit for each and every step you make in the right direction, starting right here, right now.

What We "Will Do" and "Won't Do"

In a nutshell, the Six Weeks to Sexy Abs diet consists of nutrient-dense, calorie-light, whole plant foods. Let's take a look at the basic principles of the plan.

Here is what we WILL do as part of the diet:

- Increase the amount of nutrient-dense foods we consume.
- Eliminate refined sugars from our diet.
- Decrease the amount of processed foods we eat.
- Eliminate animal products and bi-products from our diet.
- Eliminate dietary cholesterol and trans fat from our diet.
- Decrease the amount of saturated fat we consume.
- Decrease the amount of processed grains in our diet.
- Listen to our bodies and use simple techniques to control portion size.

Here is what we WILL NOT do as part of the diet:

- Calorie count.
- Replace animal products with empty-calorie foods.
- Replace animal products with highly processed foods.
- Feel hungry all the time.
- Overeat high calorie plant foods.
- Beat ourselves up if we "mess up."

Understanding why the Six Weeks to Sexy Abs Plan works is a must for you to make the commitment and stick to it. The basic principles are surprisingly simple!

The Six Weeks to Sexy Abs Plan works because it is:

Comprised of Nutrient-Dense Plant Foods

Why does having a diet filled with nutrient-dense plant foods make such a difference? Eating foods that have a high nutrient content per calorie make it possible for you to give your body what it needs in the most efficient way possible. Think of it as getting more bang for your caloric buck! Your body needs good calories, filled with essential nutrients to thrive. When you start to give your body these essentials, your body will say, "I'm finally getting everything I need! Now I can let go of the extra body fat I was clinging to!" That's precisely when your body transformation will begin.

Low In Simple Carbohydrates

The Six Weeks to Sexy Abs diet is void of processed sugars and relatively low in grains. The grains that are included are nutritious whole grains that provide you with needed energy. Although fruits are sometimes considered simple carbohydrates, when eaten whole or blended, the fiber in the fruit allows you to utilize the sugars in a healthy way. They are extremely nutrient-dense and provide you with helpful energy that your body will crave during the day, especially when you are training hard throughout the week!

Calorie Light

As I mentioned before, we will not be counting calories. Why is that? With this plan, there's no need! By following the basic guidelines, the Six Weeks to Sexy Abs diet is lower in calories than the Standard American Diet by default. Significantly lower! The calories you do consume are quality calories. We are simply cutting out empty and harmful calories, filling our bodies with more nutritious calories, and voilà, our body fat drops!

Void of Chemicals, Additives and Preservatives

The chemicals and preservatives found in the majority of products on the grocery shelves today have harmful effects, both short and long term. Artificial sweeteners confuse your body, causing sugar cravings that can really throw you off your healthy track. They can also affect brain chemistry and cause the release of insulin into the blood stream. For many people, artificial ingredients can also create digestive problems. Additionally, artificial sweeteners over time may slow our metabolism. Not worth it! Chemicals, additives and preservatives are simply no good and don't have any business in our bodies so we stay away from them as a rule.

Satisfying

The meals on the Six Weeks to Sexy Abs menu are both delicious and satisfying. The food is flavorful with a variety of textures that can help satisfy cravings (we will talk about cravings a little later). The meals are also high in fiber, which helps you feel full but does not sit "heavy" in your stomach, a feeling many people experience with meals high in meat and animal bi-products. Secondly, you won't get bored with the menu from one day to the next. The wide variety of foods, flavors and preparation techniques used will keep your taste buds interested and happy. Don't worry, the meal plan goes way beyond "rabbit food"!

Effective at Increasing Your Metabolism

Starting the day with a nutrient-packed breakfast kick-starts your metabolism. Many people skip breakfast, which has a detrimental effect on your metabolism for the rest of the day. Your body goes into "starvation mode" and does its best to preserve fat ... the very thing you don't want! This plan is structured to support an increase in your metabolic rate so that you are burning more calories more consistently, causing your extra body fat to drop.

Simple, Convenient and Customizable

The Six Weeks to Sexy Abs diet takes into consideration that most people are in need of a plan that fits their busy lifestyle. Not many of us have time to spend hours in the kitchen these days (nor do many of us want to!). The recipes on the menu are easy-to-follow, and the meal plan provides simple suggestions to save you time throughout the week, making your life as easy as possible. Following the simple guidelines and using the sample six-week meal plan to steer you down the right path, you will come out on top!

The Exercise Component

By focusing on diet, I'm in no way saying exercise isn't important. It absolutely is! Developing a strong, well-balanced musculoskeletal system is a fundamental component of basic health and well-being. Exercise also plays a key role in maintaining a healthy weight. And on top of it all, strong is sexy!

An effective exercise program that strengthens your muscles and bones, and improves your cardiovascular system, is an essential component of looking and feeling your best for years to come. The Six Weeks to Sexy Abs Plan includes an efficient and effective workout regimen designed to sculpt strong lean muscles while shedding body fat. Your success in achieving the body you want is contingent on your commitment to following the recommended diet. Remember, you can't outrun your fork!

In this day and age, most of us have access to convenient places to exercise, whether it's the gym down the street, at a park around the block or even in your own living room. There are also tons of choices when it comes to classes, trainers and exercise videos that can help guide and motivate us to work out. I'm here to encourage you to take advantage of all the resources available to you that will help you maintain an active lifestyle. I support you in finding the types of activities that not only challenge you, but also bring you a sense of accomplishment and satisfaction.

The workout regimen in the Six Weeks to Sexy Abs Plan is intense and highly effective. It's designed to burn body fat and gain lean muscle to help you get those cut abs you desire in the shortest time frame possible.

Commitment (yes, that dreaded word!) to both a workout schedule and eating plan is required to successfully change your body. Think about it though ... our commitment to exercise is only about one hour per day. What about our commitment to nutrition? We have 24 hours every day in which we must commit to making healthy food choices. Not only that, we are also overloaded with different information about what we should and shouldn't put in our mouths. Your trainer might tell you to try the Paleo diet, while your doctor tells you to lower your fat intake. You then read that a low carb, gluten-free diet is the key to losing weight. Who do you listen to? How do you even begin to get motivated to make changes when you don't know what the right changes are?

The Six Weeks to Sexy Abs Plan gives you a structure to follow. A plan that will give you results quickly and start the motivational snowball effect. Once you experience even a little bit of change in the right direction, your motivation level automatically increases. You find yourself inspired to get to the gym and cook a healthy meal. You will be on a roll in no time! All you have to do is commit and give it your all. We're talking six weeks out of a lifetime here—you got this!

Added Benefits of a Plant-Based Diet

While looking good naked may be the most outwardly obvious benefit of a healthy, plant-based diet, there are countless other reasons to go vegan. Knowing these other reasons can be added motivation for sticking with the Six Weeks to Sexy Abs Plan, so let's take a look at these added benefits now.

Prevent Disease

Whole plant foods are the most powerful weapon we have to fight disease! A plant-based diet can prevent, treat and even cure many diseases, including our top killers, heart disease and cancer. Looking at diet as our drug of choice instead of prescription medications, and understanding that more time in the kitchen now can result in less time in the hospital later, is key!

Improve How You Feel on a Daily Basis

There's a long list of potential ways you will feel better daily on a plant-based diet. You can experience a better overall mood, clearer skin, improved digestion and bowel functioning, better sleep, enhanced performance, increased concentration level ... shall I go on?

Save Animals

It's sometimes easier to feel motivated to help others even more than helping ourselves. This can be especially true when it comes to our furry friends. The conditions on the factory farms where the vast majority of farm animals are raised and killed are horrific. Eating a plant-based diet means doing your part to stop the appalling treatment of innocent creatures. Watching a video that exposes the practices that take place inside factory farms is an effective way to stay on track with your eating when you start to waiver!

Preserve the Environment

The environmental impact of raising animals for food is devastating. In fact, eliminating meat from your diet is the single most important contribution you can make to help preserve our planet. The greenhouse gases that are produced from livestock have a far more expansive impact on ozone depletion than all transportation combined. Massive amounts of natural resources are used to raise the number of cows it takes to feed just a handful of people. If these same resources were used to raise the plants that are fed directly to people, there would be no food shortages. There are plenty of informative documentaries on the topic. I encourage you to check them out and become informed on the facts that have been hidden from us for years!

Motivation and Mindset for Success

Before you begin the Six Weeks to Sexy Abs Plan, we need to get you set up to succeed! You are a unique human being and your specific needs and desires are different than any other person in the world. Developing a mindset that will keep you motivated for the next six weeks and beyond is critical. It's all about preparing for a positive experience! The answers you come up with to the following questions will empower you to find the motivation you need to change those old, stubborn, bad habits and form new good ones that will serve you better! Take some time now to write down your answers to each question. Having your answers written out on paper is essential to your success. Reviewing your answers daily can keep your mindset in success mode throughout the entire six weeks!

1. What are your goals?

In order to succeed you must have a vision of what success looks like. This takes goals. Take a minute now to write down your goal(s). What difference do you want to see six weeks from now?

2. What is your driving force to change your unhealthy habits?

When it comes to change, part of the process involves understanding that in order to change, we must be uncomfortable! It's not easy to be uncomfortable, and that's why we often fall back into old, bad habits—because they are comfortable. No more! What is your driving force for change? What is it that will make this time be different than attempts at change in the past? Identify those reasons now.

3. What is your "Personal Power Statement"?

I encourage you to develop phrases, or mantras, that you can turn to when you are feeling challenged. I call them personal power statements. It may seem silly at first, but it can really work! You can have one or multiple statements for different situations. The idea is to empower yourself when you begin to slip into a victim mentality, which we all do at times. Here are a couple I use:

"It takes only one person to change my life. Me! I have the power!"

"Everything I ever wanted is on the other side of fear. Fear is not going to stop me, I can do this!"

"I'm not on a diet ... I'm eating according to my goals. I will reach my goals!"

"This too shall pass."

"What others think of me is none of my business!"

"Letting go is the key to happiness."

4. Who will make up your support team?

Being proactive in putting together a support team is a must. The people that surround you can be a great help or a hindrance. Talk to your coworkers, friends and family ahead of time about the journey you are embarking on for the next six weeks. It will make your life easier if your coworker stops offering you a bagel with cream cheese in the mornings! You will find that many people will be inspired by what you are doing and even want to join you! In addition, find support from people with experience living a healthy plant-based lifestyle. Social media and online chat rooms are great for this! There is such a vast wealth of support online from organizations and individuals who are passionate about eating clean and green!

What to Expect

Let's touch on what you can expect during the six weeks you are on the plan. First off, everyone reacts differently, both physically and mentally, to the dietary changes you're about to make. There are a ton of different factors that can come into play, many of them having to do with what your diet has consisted of up until now. Are you already highly plant-based or are you a meat-eater ready to take on a challenge for change? Are you a cheese-oholic? What about a sugar addict?

If your body is accustomed to a diet heavy in animal products, sugar and/or processed foods, it's going to get a bit of a shock. A good shock—but a shock nonetheless!

Some people feel better almost immediately. The "heavy" feeling they carried around daily vanishes and they feel lighter and more energetic. Their digestive system welcomes the high doses of plant food and begins to function better right off the bat.

For others, there is more of an adjustment period in which the body must detoxify from years of a diet high in toxins. This is quite the task! It sometimes leaves people feeling achy, irritable and crappy for a few days, sometimes even a couple weeks. It's important to realize that this is a possibility before you begin the Six Weeks to Sexy Abs Meal Plan because these symptoms could feel completely defeating if you are unaware of the reasons behind them.

Cravings are often a concern—understandably! Cravings are tricky. Sometimes they come from a place of food addiction. Just like when a drug addict goes through withdrawal and craves their drug of choice. Think of sugar as a drug. In fact, it's been said that sugar is more addictive than heroin! Bottom line, the cravings you may get during the plan may be caused by withdrawal and have nothing to do with what your body "needs."

When it comes to cravings for foods outside the guidelines of the Six Weeks to Sexy Abs Meal Plan, the trick is going to be substitutions. Think about what it is, exactly, that you're craving. Is it the "fleshy" texture of a steak? Time to cook up a Portobello "steak"! Craving a chocolate bar? Don't worry, check out the dessert recipes and whip up a batch of chocolate mousse made from cacao, avocado and dates! Sound a little crazy? Just wait until you try it! I promise you'll be more than pleasantly surprised. The recipes in this book offer a wide range of different textures and flavors so you can tackle any prevailing craving.

Last, let's discuss "messing up." This concern can easily get you in trouble so let's nip it in the bud. It all comes down to staying focused on the positive. I want you to give yourself credit for each and every step you make in the right direction. After every meal you make, every workout you complete, take the time to acknowledge your accomplishments. Also, recognize that every moment is a new opportunity to take a positive step forward, even if you feel you took a step backward the moment before. We are human. We make mistakes. Realizing that mistakes are simply learning experiences, accepting yourself no matter what, and living in the present moment is key to empowering yourself to stick with the program.

CHAPTER II

THE SIX-WEEK PLAN OF *Action*

OVERVIEW

So here we are, time for action! The Six Weeks to Sexy Abs Plan is a simple, practical, easy-to-follow formula. Take a look!

	MON	TUES	WED	THURS	FRI	SAT	SUN
BREAKFAST	Super Smoothie	Super Smoothie	Super Smoothie	Super Smoothie	Super Smoothie	Badass Breakfast	Bangin' Brunch
LUNCH	Sexy Salad (Entrée)	Luscious Leftovers	Sexy Salad (Entrée)	Luscious Leftovers	Sexy Salad (Entrée)	Luscious Leftovers	
SNACK	Fruit	Fruit	Fruit	Fruit	Fruit	Fruit	Fruit
DINNER	Sensual Soup & Side	Mighty Meal	Sensual Soup & Side	Mighty Meal	Sensual Soup & Side	Mighty Meal	Mighty Meal
TREAT (optional)	X	X	Tantalizing Treat	X	X	X	Tantalizing Treat
FLUIDS	Drink plenty every day!						
WORKOUT	Cross-Train (full body focus)	Cardio + Yoga	Cross-Train (upper body focus)	Cardio	Cross-Train (lower body focus)	Yoga + Cardio	Off/Rest

THE FORMULA

The Six Weeks to Sexy Abs formula was designed for practicality, effectiveness and satisfaction. Having a routine that you can follow each week is key to staying consistent and getting results. Keep in mind that the formula is based on a typical workweek, so if you have a different type of schedule, you may need to make some adjustments. If you have a job that has you working on Saturday and Sunday for example, and your "weekend" is Monday and Tuesday, then adjust the formula accordingly. As long as you understand the guidelines of the program, you're good to go! Now let's delve into each component of the Six Weeks to Sexy Abs Plan.

BREAKFAST

SUPER SMOOTHIE

I call these super smoothies for a reason: They are all packed with super foods! For the purpose of this meal plan, "super foods" can be defined as "whole plant foods that are especially high in important vitamins, minerals, antioxidants and/or other phytonutrients." Each smoothie consists of multiple super foods. It's a perfect way to start the day because:

- It can be created in a matter of minutes. This is particularly important for most of us during the workweek. Lack of time is often the reason we get off to a poor start to the day nutritionally speaking.

- Blending a bunch of super foods together is the most effective, surefire way to pack your body full of a wide variety of vital nutrients, starting your day off right. Unlike juicing, blending fruits and vegetables preserves all the nutrients and fiber from the food and allows us to ingest and absorb them.

The sample menu gives you great smoothie recipes to try, and when it comes time to create your own, you'll be ready!

ADDITIONAL PROTEIN OPTION

If you have a ton of muscle already that you want to maintain or are trying to gain more muscle, as opposed to strengthening and toning the muscle you already have, you may need to increase your protein intake. On this plan, you can do this by simply adding a scoop of protein powder to your morning smoothie, or having a scoop blended or shaken with water or vegan milk during the day, preferably immediately following your workout.

There are many whole foods–based vegan protein powders on the market you can choose from. The protein powder you choose should be whole plant food–based, non-GMO and organic. It should not contain any "isolates" such as "soy protein isolate," and I recommend simply staying away from soy protein powder altogether. The meal plan already includes soy in other forms, which is great for you in moderation, but there's no need to overdo it. Also stay away from products containing added sugars, preservatives or other unnecessary ingredients. There are many quality complete protein powders (containing all the branched chain amino acids, or BCAAs) available made from hemp, pea, rice and other combinations of a variety of whole plant foods. Most are sold in both individual packets as well as large containers so that you are able to give them a try and find the ones that you enjoy most.

BADASS BREAKFAST

By the time the weekend rolls around, you'll probably be ready for some traditional breakfast-type of food. Hot cereals make a great choice. You can prepare them with all sorts of different combinations of whole grains, seeds, nuts and fruit. That's just one option of many, though. The breakfast recipes in this plan will give you many great ideas for badass breakfasts.

BANGIN' BRUNCH

Sunday says brunch! We let loose a bit on Sundays and explore some awesome brunch-worthy meals. The idea is for you to get to eat delicious food that satisfies your cravings for all sorts of animal-based foods you may miss when trying out a vegan menu for the first time. Many of these meals take a bit longer to prepare than the breakfast recipes. It's Sunday Funday—take your time and have fun with the experience!

LUNCH

SEXY SALAD

This is a meal-worthy salad containing both greens and a variety of other vegetables, many of them raw—as the base—with legumes, nuts, seeds, fruit and/or whole grains for added protein and useful carbs. These salads are nutrient-dense and satisfying. They are eaten for lunch largely because they are convenient to pack and eat during lunchtime, no matter where you are. Depending on the salad, you may want to keep the dressing separate, adding it right before you eat so that it won't be soggy. The sexy salad recipes included in the meal plan will show you just how enticing and fulfilling a salad can be!

LUSCIOUS LEFTOVERS

Time to give leftovers a makeover. This is where we get practical and say, "Twice is nice!" I'm all about creating awesome new dishes, but I also know that practicality is the key to consistency. Throwing together a lunch using food you've already prepared takes all of five minutes. It saves time, energy and money. This plan calls for three days in which you eat leftovers for lunch. It's okay to adjust the formula to include more leftover meals throughout the week if that works best for you. All of the recipes in this book are nutritious, so you really can't go wrong eating them twice.

SNACK

FRUIT

There's no better snack during the day than fruit: simple, nutritious and delicious! By eating only one type of fruit for your snack, you make it easy for your body to digest, leaving you with only positive energy and enough food in your tummy to tide you over until your next meal. Depending on your schedule, you will either eat a snack between breakfast and lunch, or between lunch and dinner. It's your choice. Keep in mind that berries are especially good for you and are lower in calories than most other types of fruit. Also, remember that variety is key!

DINNER

SENSUAL SOUP & SIDE

The soup and side dish combos contain a variety of vegetables, legumes, nuts, seeds, fruits, grain-like seeds and/or whole grains to create a healthy, balanced meal. The soup recipes in this book will make enough soup to last for at least two meals. You have the option of eating the leftovers as another meal during the same week (many soups even taste better the second day), in which case you would store the leftovers in the refrigerator, or freeze them for a meal weeks down the road. Soups are accompanied by a simple side to complete the meal and leave you feeling happy and content. Some of the soups are so filling that you may not feel you need a side. That's fine! There's nothing wrong with eating soup as your main course, especially when it's extra hearty, so feel free to adjust the meal by leaving out the side dish. Many of the soup recipes in this book are blended. Healthy, blended soups make an especially great dinner because they are easier to digest and can be helpful when it comes to getting a good night of sleep.

MIGHTY MEAL

These dinner dishes are primarily made up of cooked vegetables and whole food–based protein. Grain-like seeds such as quinoa and nutrient-dense whole grains can be incorporated, but in moderation in order to keep evening carb intake lower before bed. These dishes are both simple and gratifying. Many recipes give you shortcut options that can significantly cut down on your time in the kitchen, but these shortcuts can also cut down on the freshness of the meal. Many of the shortcuts involve store-bought sauces and dressings, and pre-cut frozen vegetables. The benefit of making sauces and dressings from scratch is that you can control exactly what's in them. Store-bought sauces and dressings, even the organic ones, can often include an ingredient or two that you would not have chosen to use if you were making it yourself. Don't sweat it though. If you are following the basic guidelines of the meal plan and using a premade sauce is going to make your life easier, then go for it! Many of these mighty meals will also make perfect luscious leftovers. Some can even be frozen for use a week or two down the road.

DESSERT

TANTALIZING TREATS

These desserts give you a chance to satisfy your sweet tooth while being true to a healthy, plant-based diet. The base ingredients in these sweet treats are whole fruits, nuts and seeds. We add a touch of pure maple syrup here and there, and semi-sweet chocolate on occasion, but that's about it. There's simply no room or need for refined sugars during these six weeks. You have a goal to reach! Don't worry, though—with these sweet treats you won't even miss junk food. And if you are one of those rare people that lack a sweet tooth, you are certainly free to skip the treat. It's simply a bonus available if you want to take advantage.

WATER/FLUIDS

WATER

Drink a lot of water and check out your pee. Yes, seriously! Generally, you will know if you aren't getting enough water if your urine is dark. The clearer it is, the more hydrated you are. You lose water through sweat when you are working out, so make sure you are replacing that water by drinking more before, during and after your workout. Also, we sometimes mistake thirst for hunger, so if you feel hungry, first drink a glass of water, wait ten minutes, and the hunger you thought you felt may very well be gone. Another good tip is to keep a glass of water by your bedside. When your alarm goes off in the morning, roll over and drink that water. It's an awesome way to start the day.

COFFEE/TEA

Although it's not part of the meal plan, don't worry coffee-drinkers, you don't have to give up your morning cup o' Joe! Herbal tea, especially green and white tea, is recommended as part of the Six Weeks to Sexy Abs Plan. Herbal tea has many health benefits and is a great way to increase your fluid intake while adding flavor and interest (sometimes plain water just doesn't "do it" for us). In fact, both tea and coffee "count" as part of your tally for water intake throughout the day. It's what you put into your coffee that we have to focus on. If you like your coffee or tea sweet, use stevia instead of sugar or artificial sweeteners. Keep in mind that a little stevia goes a long way. If you add too much, it will taste bitter. If you usually drink your coffee with milk, creamer or half and half, you can replace it with a vegan substitute. Drinking your coffee black is the healthier option, but with all the other healthy changes you are making during these six weeks, if a serving of vegan creamer is something that you love, I say go ahead and enjoy it. Buy the "regular" flavored option since the flavored options tend to have more sugar.

ALCOHOL

Unfortunately, alcohol is not going to help your cause. If you are not a drinker anyway, great! Continue on your path of abstinence. If, however, you enjoy a glass of wine at dinner, cocktails on the weekends with friends or beer while watching your sports, you have a choice to make. Giving up alcohol for six weeks will help you reach your goals faster, plain and simple. If you are unwilling to give up alcohol all together during the plan, I've devised a few rules to help you drink in a way that will hurt you the least. First of all, no matter what alcohol you drink, moderation is key. Having a glass of wine with dinner on the weekends is one thing; downing a bottle every few days is a whole other thing! Don't!

When it comes to cocktails, the rule is simple. No mixers. Mixers will ruin you! Use soda water, lemons and limes to mix with your liquor. If you need some sweetness, you can add stevia. Put a stevia packet in your purse when you go out!

Look at alcohol as empty calories that must be burned off. Think about it in these terms: For every one and a half calories of beer you drink, it will take at least one burpee to burn it off. If you've ever done a burpee, you know that even a set of 10 will have your heart pumping hard! So take an average beer containing 150 calories: You will have to perform over 100 burpees to burn off those calories! Yikes!

The last thing to keep in mind is that alcohol dehydrates you, and unlike coffee, it does not count toward your water intake tally. It actually increases your requirement for water. So for every serving of alcohol you drink, consume an extra glass of water. By alternating alcohol with water, you will also have an easier time drinking at a slower pace and keeping your alcohol intake moderate.

NUTRITION GUIDELINES

Below is a guide of approximate food goals to hit, on average, during the six weeks of the plan. The precise number of portions per day that will help you drop body fat is dependent on many factors. For one, the numbers will vary based on your goal weight. For example, a 135-pound (61-kg) woman with the goal of reaching 125-pounds (57-kg), will need to consume fewer portions than a 200-pound

FOOD GROUP	PORTION SIZE
LEAFY GREEN VEGETABLES: 2+ PORTIONS/DAY—THE MORE THE BETTER!	1 portion of raw leafy greens = 1 grabbing handful, chopped 1 portion of cooked leafy greens = ½ cup (30 g), chopped
NON-LEAFY VEGETABLES (EXCLUDING WHITE POTATOES): 3+ PORTIONS OF NON-STARCHY VEGETABLES/DAY AND 0–2 PORTIONS OF STARCHY VEGETABLES/DAY SUCH AS SWEET POTATO AND CORN	1 portion of raw vegetables = 1 cup (80 g), chopped 1 portion of cooked vegetables = ⅔ cup (100 g), chopped
FRUIT: 3–5 PORTIONS/DAY	1 portion of fresh fruit = 1 cup (125 g), chopped, or equivalent to 1 apple 1 portion of dried fruit= ¼ cup (32 g)
LEGUMES: 2–4 PORTIONS/DAY	1 portion = ½ cup (125 g), canned or cooked
NUTS/SEEDS: 2–4 PORTIONS/DAY	1 portion of nuts (½ an ounce [15 g]) = 12 almonds, 9 cashews, 7 walnut halves, 4 Brazil nuts, 10 pecan halves 1 portion of nut butter = 1 tablespoon (4 g)
GRAIN-LIKE SEEDS (QUINOA, BUCKWHEAT, AMARANTH, MILLET): 0–2 PORTIONS/DAY	1 portion = ½ cup (90 g), cooked
AVOCADO: 1–2 PORTIONS/DAY	1 portion = ½ a small avocado
WHOLE GRAINS: 0–1 PORTIONS/DAY	1 portion = ½ cup (75 g), cooked
APPROVED OILS: 0–2 PORTIONS/DAY	1 portion = 1 tbsp (15 ml)
WATER/FLUIDS: MINIMUM = BODYWEIGHT X 0.5 + 12 OZ (355 ML) FOR EVERY 30 MIN. EXERCISE = OZ (ML)/DAY	Example: 140 lb (64 kg) x 0.5 = 70 oz (2 L) plus 45 minutes exercise, an extra 18 oz (0.5 L) = 88 oz (2.5 L) water for the day

(90-kg) man with the goal weight of 185-pounds (84-kg). The numbers also depend on your activity level and metabolic rate. These guidelines will give you an idea as to the proportion of each food group to consume on a daily basis. When it comes to portion control, I have a simple rule of thumb. Eat slowly and stop eating when you feel 80% full. Using smaller plates, bowls and silverware can actually help you follow that rule. Your brain will be tricked into thinking you're eating more food if there's less empty room on your plate or in your bowl, and you will eat slower with a smaller fork or spoon in hand.

THE RECIPES

The recipes in this book are designed to be quick and simple enough to follow exactly, yet flexible enough to be altered to fit your taste and schedule. The following information will help you get the most out of the sample menus and recipes.

Prep Day

It's helpful to have a "prep day" at the beginning of the week. Prepare anything and everything that you can prepare ahead of time. This is especially important if you are limited in time and energy during the week. Every bit of work you can get done on prep day will make the rest of your week easier. It's also a great time to take a look at the slow cooker recipes because you will need to prepare those either the night before, or the morning of the day you plan to eat the soup.

Prep day can include:

Pressing tofu: Most of the tofu dishes recommend using pressed tofu (page 43). This plays a huge role in reaching the desired texture. Often people think of tofu as "mushy," which can be a turnoff! Removing the water from extra-firm tofu does the trick to take care of this issue.

Cooking whole grains/grain like-seeds: Take a look at the type of whole grains and grain-like seeds that you will be using during the week and go ahead and cook up a big batch. They will store just fine in the fridge in a sealed container all week long. Make sure to take note on whether the grain is being used in a savory dish or sweet dish. For savory dishes, cooking the grain in vegetable broth is a great way to add flavor. However, for sweet dishes, using plain water is a must.

Chopping vegetables: Opening the fridge and seeing a container of ready-to-cook, chopped veggies is inviting, while seeing whole vegetables can seem daunting, especially at the end of a busy day. Chop as many veggies you can on prep day and place them in sealed containers, and I promise you will appreciate it all week long!

Grocery Lists

The following staple grocery list contains the spices, seasoning, condiments and other foods that you will need to buy only once—if you don't already have them in your kitchen—to last you at least the entire six weeks of the plan, and likely beyond. Most of the items on these lists can be found at any typical health food market, and many will be on the shelves at regular grocery stores as well. Another option you have with many of the items is to order online. You can find products such as organic hemp and chia seeds on Amazon and other online retailers, so go ahead and place those orders! Items with an "*" are those you may be less familiar with. You can find a description of each on pages 200–202.

Once you've stocked up on these items, you can begin the Six Weeks to Sexy Abs Plan. As you go through the Plan, you will find a grocery list for each week, which will not include the items on the staples list. No need to get overwhelmed looking at the entire meal plan, and all the grocery lists at once. Simply take it one week at a time, without getting ahead of yourself, and you'll be golden!

GROCERY LIST—STAPLES

NUTS/SEEDS/BERRIES

- Almond butter
- Chia seeds, raw*
- Flax meal, raw*
- Hemp seeds, hulled, raw*
- Peanut butter (optional)
- Sesame seeds (black and/or white)
- Tahini*

GRAINS/GRAIN-LIKE SEEDS

- Buckwheat*
- Farro*
- Millet*
- Quinoa, sprouted if possible*
- Rolled Oats

SPICES

- Bay leaves, dried
- Cayenne pepper (optional)
- Chili powder
- Chives, dried
- Cinnamon, ground
- Cornstarch
- Cracked black pepper (with grinder)
- Cumin powder
- Curry powder
- Garlic powder
- Ginger powder
- Himalayan or Celtic sea salt
- Herbamare seasoning*
- Italian seasoning blend
- Mustard powder
- Onion powder
- Oregano, dried
- Paprika
- Red pepper flakes (optional)
- Thyme, dried
- Turmeric powder
- Wasabi powder or paste

CONDIMENTS/SEASONINGS

- Apple cider vinegar
- Bragg Liquid Aminos*
- Cacao nibs or vegan chocolate chips*
- Capers
- Coconut flakes, unsweetened
- Dijon mustard
- Garlic, minced (in a jar)
- Hot sauce (optional)
- Lemon juice, not from concentrate
- Lime juice, not from concentrate
- Mayo, vegan version (e.g., Follow Your Heart's Vegenaise, Beyond Meat's Just Mayo)
- Nutritional yeast*
- Pure vanilla extract
- Raw cacao powder*
- Red and white wine vinegar
- Salsa
- Stevia powder*

OILS

- Extra virgin olive oil (EVOO)
- High-heat cooking oils: grape seed oil, sesame oil, refined coconut oil and/or avocado oil
- Unrefined coconut oil and/or vegan buttery spread (e.g., Earth Balance)

PROTEIN PRODUCTS & SMOOTHIE ADDITIONS

- 7 Lean Protein
- Amla powder* (optional)
- Maca powder* (optional)
- Vegan protein powder of choice (RAW Protein, 22 Days Protein Powder, Sun Warrior, Nutiva Hemp Protein, Vega Performance Protein, BalanceDiet)

MISCELLANEOUS

- Explore Asian brand bean pasta (edamame and mung bean fettuccini and adjuki bean spaghetti)

*See pages 200–202 for more information.

Buying Organic

It's best to buy organic and locally farmed foods. The recipes don't specify "organic" because there's no need for you to see "organic" hundreds of times. Some produce is more important than others to choose organic. The Environmental Working Group (www.ewg.org) puts out a list of the "Clean Fifteen" (foods least likely to hold pesticide residues), and the "Dirty Dozen" (foods most likely to be contaminated with hazardous pesticide residue), updated every year. This is a good place to start if you are on a tight budget or there is limited availability of organic food in your market, to help you make informed decisions.

Substitutions/Conversions

The recipes contain many options to make it easy to customize based on your time restrictions and ingredients you are more or less likely to have available to use. See page 198 for common substitutions you may want or need to make, such as vegan milk choices, fresh vs. dried herbs, and cooking oil options.

THE WORKOUTS

The supplemental workout plan is intense yet balanced, and totally do-able! The combination of cross-training and cardio throughout the week will not only burn tons of calories (many of which are fat calories), but will also help you gain lean, toned muscles. Sticking to the training regimen plays a huge role in increasing your metabolism. Simply put, the more lean muscle you have, the more calories you burn all the time, even when you're just sitting around on the couch!

The following explanations will give you the guidelines you need to get the most out of your training routine during the six weeks of the plan.

Cross-Training

Cross-training is a method of training that is highly variable in the ways you move your body, the muscles you use and the amount and type of stress you place on your body. You incorporate all types of exercises into these sessions. You perform some movements that spike your heart rate to the max, some that involve heavier lifting with a lower number of repetitions, lighter weight with high repetition and lots of functional movements. I've incorporated cross-training heavily into the workout plan because it is an effective method to:

- Build muscle strength
- Build muscle endurance
- Improve cardiovascular system
- Improve overall conditioning and fitness level
- Burn a crap-load of calories
- Increase metabolism
- Include functional movements
- Prevent overuse injuries

In the Six Weeks to Sexy Abs Plan, cross-training is scheduled for three sessions per week. Each session has a slightly different focus. Let's discuss each.

Full Body Focused: Your cross-training routine on "full body day" will focus on total body movements and exercises that build core strength. My top three all-time favorite exercises that fall into these categories are:

- burpees
- plank variations
- mountain climbers

These three exercises are so effective, and utilize so many important muscles, that you can incorporate them into your workouts every single week, and they will continue to help you toward your goals.

Upper Body Focused: Your routine on this day will include more exercises that build muscle strength in your upper body rather than your lower body. This doesn't mean you won't do full body exercises, it simply means the emphasis of the workout as a whole will be on your back, chest, shoulders, biceps and/or triceps.

When planning your workouts, it's important to consider muscle balance. A muscle imbalance is created when one muscle group becomes stronger than its opposing muscle group, and it can cause aches and injuries. Lower back pain is so common in large part due to a person's back being weaker and more stretched out than his/her chests (consider back and chest opposing groups). If you, like so many people, sit hunched over a desk all day, every day, you'll develop poor posture. Your shoulders will roll inward and your chest muscles will shorten and tighten. As your chest tightens, your back stretches, becomes weaker and creates mechanical damage. This damage results in back pain. It's therefore super important to incorporate regular back strengthening exercises, including lower back specific exercises, into your exercise program to prevent and treat such imbalances.

Top effective upper body exercises include:

- pull-ups (back)
- chin-ups (back and biceps)
- push-ups (chest)
- diver push-ups (triceps)
- handstand push-ups (advanced, but can be modified) (shoulders)

Lower Body Focused: Your routine on this day will focus more on exercises that build your lower body strength including your glutes (think shelf booty!), hamstrings, quadriceps and calves. It's important to not only do exercises that work both legs together, but also those that work your legs individually to help develop balance and coordination. This helps ensure that one leg is not doing more work than the other, causing muscle imbalance and leading to pain and injury.

Top effective lower body exercises include:

- squat variations
- lunge variations
- pistols (advanced but can be modified)
- box jumps

Cardio: Cardiovascular exercise strengthens your heart, improves endurance, builds stamina and burns calories. A heart rate monitor is an essential tool for you to get the most out of your cardio workouts. Monitoring your heart rate allows you to control the "zone" you are working in throughout the session. Staying in the moderate intensity zone (70–80% of your maximum heart rate) and pushing into the high intensity zone (80–90% of your maximum heart rate) for interval periods is a great way to burn fat and improve your VO_2 Max (maximum oxygen intake/lung capacity).

The easiest way to figure out your target heart rate is by using an app on your phone or tablet that calculates it for you when you enter the requested information. You will need to provide your age and resting heart rate. Get the most accurate resting heart rate by counting the beats in one full minute upon waking up in the morning, before you have done much moving around.

You can also manually calculate your target zones with the following formula:

208 – (0.7 x age) = maximum heart rate

maximum heart rate – resting heart rate = heart rate reserve

heart rate reserve x training percentage + resting heart rate = target heart rate

Here is an example using a 35-year-old woman with a resting heart rate of 65.

208 – (0.7 x 35 [age]) = 183.5

183.45 – 65 = 118.5

118.5 x 0.70 + 65 = 148 (rounded)

118.5 x 0.80 + 65 = 160 (rounded)

118.5 x 0.90 + 65 = 172 (rounded)

Her moderate intensity zone is around 148–160, and her high intensity zone is approximately 160–172 beats per minute.

You don't have to spend big money on a fancy heart rate monitor with all the bells and whistles. As long as it accurately shows your real-time heart rate so you can monitor it throughout your workout, it will work. If having special features such as tracking your progress over multiple workouts or having GPS to map your runs will motivate you, then by all means, go for it!

Some effective methods of cardio are:

• jogging
• walking or jogging on an incline
• cycling
• jumping rope
• cardio kickboxing
• stair climbing
• elliptical-type machine (great if you have joint issues)

Yoga: Spending all your time building strength and tightening your muscles will serve you best if you balance it with significant muscle stretching and lengthening. Yoga is an effective method of ensuring you are balancing your training regimen with both. Take a class or watch a video and do it in your living room—it's up to you.

You may already enjoy yoga, or you may try it and take pleasure in it immediately. Awesome, keep it up! However, if you are like me, you may not take to yoga right away. It took me years to climb on board the yoga train! I was given a wake-up call, a severe injury, and was forced to lay off the intense Muay Thai kickboxing and take on rehab. Before long, yoga became part of my rehabilitation. Whereas before I always made an excuse, yoga was no longer an option that I could ignore.

I don't want you to experience a wake-up call like mine! Prevention is where it's at. Not only can yoga help prevent physical injuries, it can also help us get better at appreciating life. As Zen Buddhist Thich Nhat Hanh said, "Life can be found only in the present moment ... If we are not fully ourselves, truly in the present moment, we miss everything." I encourage you to put the excuses aside and commit to practicing yoga twice a week for these six weeks and see what happens!

On pages 29–31 you'll find a sample week of workouts that fit the Six Weeks to Sexy Abs formula. Unlike eating meals, your workout routine greatly depends on your current level of fitness. Your workouts need to challenge you and push you past your comfort zone, because that's how progress is made. I will never forget the words my fitness instructor mentor used to yell out during her classes. "In order to change you must be ..." and then the class would belt out the answer, "Uncomfortable!" Note that there is a line between discomfort and injury, and it's a line you must determine for yourself during each and every workout. The sample workouts provide two versions of each routine, one that will challenge the average "advanced" and one that will challenge the average "beginner/intermediate" level person. You will need to tweak the amount of weight and the repetitions to meet your individual needs, but having this sample will help you get the hang of the formula the first week so you can better follow it for the following five weeks. You got this!

SAMPLE WEEK OF WORKOUTS

Advanced Cross-Training Monday (Full Body)

Active stretching to warm up for 5 minutes

Round 1

- 50 air squats to overhead dumbbell press with 5–10 lb (2.3–4.6 kg) dumbbells
- 10 burpees
- Plank hold 1 minute
- Jump rope, 30 double-unders or 100 singles
- Recover/rest 90 seconds

Round 2

- 40 air squat to overhead dumbbell press with 8–15 lb (3.6–6.8 kg) dumbbells
- 15 burpees
- Plank hold 1 minute
- Jump rope, 30 double-unders or 100 singles
- Recover/rest 90 seconds

Round 3

- 30 air squats to overhead dumbbell press with 10–20 lb (4.6–9.1 kg) dumbbells
- 20 burpees
- Plank hold 1 minute
- Jump rope, 30 double-unders or 100 singles

Static stretching for 5 minutes

Intermediate Cross-Training Monday (Full Body)

Active stretching to warm up for 5 minutes

Round 1

- 30 air squats to overhead press with 3–5 lb (1.4–2.3 kg) dumbbells
- 10 burpees (option to modify)
- Plank hold 30–45 seconds
- Jump rope 1 minute (modification: pretend to jump rope)
- Recover/rest 90 seconds

Round 2

- 25 squats to overhead press with 5–8 lb (2.3–3.6 kg) dumbbells
- 12 burpees (option to modify)
- Plank hold 30–45 seconds
- Jump rope 1 minute (modification: pretend to jump rope)
- Recover/rest 90 seconds

Round 3

- 20 squats to overhead press with 8–12 lb (3.6–5.4 kg) dumbbells
- 15 burpees
- Plank hold 45 seconds
- Jump rope 1 minute (modification: pretend to jump rope)

Static stretching for 5 minutes

Cardio Tuesday

Jog 45–60 minutes, heart rate staying in target zone the majority of the time. Start with a 5-minute brisk walk to warm up and end with static stretching.

Or, Elliptical machine for 45 minutes, heart rate staying in target zone for the majority of the time. Finish with 5 minutes of static stretching.

Advanced Cross-Training Wednesday (Upper Body Focused)

Active stretching to warm up for 5 minutes

Complete 3 rounds of the following

- Walking push-ups, x 10 forward and 10 back
- Pull-ups (assisted or jumping pull-ups as modification), x 10-15
- Switching plyo-lunges (no weight), x 20 total
- 30 second recovery/rest

Complete 3 Rounds of the following

- Bent-over tricep kick-backs with 8–15 lb (3.6–6.8 kg) dumbbells, x 20
- 5 bicep curls with 12–25 lb (5.4–11.3 kg) dumbbells to one burpee, x 5
- Mountain Climbers (CrossFit style), x 30
- 30 second recovery/rest

Static stretching for 5 minutes

Beginner/Intermediate Cross-Training Wednesday (Upper Body Focused)

Active stretching to warm up for 5 minutes

Complete 3 rounds of the following

- Push-ups (modification: on knees), x 10-15
- Assisted pull-up machine, x 10–15
- Alternating back-stepping lunges (no weight), x 20 total
- 30 second recovery/rest

Complete 3 Rounds of the following

- Bent-over tricep kick-backs with 5–8 lb (2.3–3.6 kg) dumbbells, x 20
- 5 bicep curls with 5–15 lb (2.3–6.8 kg) dumbbells to one burpee (option to modify), x 5
- Mountain Climbers (CrossFit style), x 10
- 30 second recovery/rest

Static stretching for 5 minutes

Yoga Wednesday

Class at a studio or using a video at home

Cardio Thursday

Stair climbing 40–60 minutes, heart rate staying in target zone the majority of the time

Advanced Cross-Training Friday (Lower Body Focused)

Active stretching to warm up for 5+ minutes

5 rounds of the following

- Walking lunges, holding 10–20 lb (4.5–9 kg) dumbbells, x 30. Each round increase the dumbbell weight
- Squat rolls, x 20 (holding light dumbbells makes them easier if necessary)
- Dead lifts holding 12–25 lb (5.4–11.3 kg) dumbbells, x 20. Each round increase the dumbbell weight
- Butterfly sit-ups, x 20
- Rest 45 seconds

Static stretching for 5+ minutes

Beginner/Intermediate Cross-Training Friday (Lower Body Focused)

Active stretching to warm up for 5+ minutes

5 rounds of the following

- Walking lunges, holding 5–10 lb (2.3–4.5 kg) dumbbells, x 20. Each round increase the dumbbell weight
- Ski Squats x 10, holding 5 lb (2.3 kg) dumbbells
- Dead lifts holding 8–12 lb (3.6–5.4 kg) dumbbells, x 20. Each round increase the dumbbell weight
- Butterfly sit-ups, x 20
- Rest 45 seconds

Static stretching for 5+ minutes

Cardio Saturday

3 Rounds staying in target zone for the majority of the time

- Incline walk 10 minutes
- Jump rope 5 minutes

OR

- Incline walk 45 minutes

Yoga Saturday

Class at a studio or using a video at home

WEEK 1

I'm psyched for you to start your first week! Before you begin with Day 1, you'll need to take a trip to the grocery store with the staple grocery list in hand. Remember, the staple grocery list is composed of the foods you can buy once and they'll last you at minimum six weeks. At first glance it may seem long and taunting, but take a closer look. Many of the items you may already have so you can check those off before you head to the store.

OVERVIEW

	MON	TUES	WED	THURS	FRI	SAT	SUN
BREAKFAST	Perfect Pear Smoothie	Coco-nana Smoothie	Beet This! Smoothie	Warrior-Worthy Smoothie	Blueberry Bonanza Smoothie	Apple Abs of Steel Oatmeal Bowl	Southwest Tofu Scramble & Fresh Grapefruit Juice
LUNCH	Color-Me-Bad Chopped Salad	Luscious Leftovers	Italian Cannellini Bean and Fennel Salad	Luscious Leftovers	Taste of Mexico Bowl	Luscious Leftovers	
SNACK	Fresh Fruit of Choice	Fresh Fruit of Choice	Fresh Fruit of Choice	Fresh Fruit of Choice	Fresh Fruit of Choice	Fresh Fruit of Choice	Fresh Fruit of Choice
DINNER	Cauliflower for Cut Abs Soup & Easy Lima Beans	Muay Thai Zucchini Noodles	Seductive Split Pea Soup & Stovetop Tomatoes	Curry Me Home & Veg Stir Fry	Cool Cucumber Dill Soup & Quinoa with Sweet Green Peas	Tahini-Topped Roasted Cauliflower Florets & Grilled Tempeh	Steamy Spaghetti Squash Marinara
TREAT	X	X	Chia-ocolate Pudding	X	X	X	Crazy for Coconut Bites
WORKOUT	Cross-Train (full body focus)	Cardio + Yoga	Cross-Train (upper body focus)	Cardio	Cross-Train (Lower Body Focus)	Yoga + Cardio	Off/Rest

GROCERY LIST - WEEK 1

LIQUIDS

- Coconut water (½ cup [120 ml])
- Vegan milk of choice, unsweetened plain (1 large carton)
- Vegetable broth (64 oz [1.9 L])

FRUIT

- Apple (1)
- Bananas (3–4)
- Beets (1)
- Coconut meat (½ cup [40 g]), optional
- Grapefruit (2-3)
- Lemon (1)
- Orange (1)
- Pear (1)
- Frozen blueberries (1½ cups [225 g])
- Frozen strawberries (5 berries)
- Goji berries (2 tbsp [30 g])
- Dates, Medjool (10)
- Raisins (¼ cup [35 g])
- Fruits of choice for snacks

LEAFY GREENS

- Romaine (3 oz [85 g])
- Italian blend mixed greens (3 handfuls)
- Kale (1 leaf), optional

VEGETABLES

- Baby bok choy (1 cup [55 g])
- Fennel (¾ cup [165 g] chopped)
- Cauliflower (2 heads)
- Celery (4 stalks)
- Cucumber (2)
- Baby spinach (5–6 handfuls)
- Yellow onion (2½)
- Red onion, optional (¼)
- Red bell pepper (2)
- Yellow bell pepper (½)
- Green bell pepper (½)
- Tomato (1)
- Cherry tomatoes (2 cups [480 g])
- Carrots (½ lb [225 g])
- White mushrooms (one 8-oz [225-g] package)
- Jalapeño (¼), optional
- Green onion (2 stalks)
- Avocado (1)
- Zucchini (3)
- Summer yellow squash (3)
- Spaghetti squash (1)
- Snow peas (⅓ cup [45 g])
- Frozen lima beans (1 cup [255 g])
- Frozen green peas (½ cup [125 g])
- Baby corn, canned (⅓ cup [45 g])
- Black olives (¼ cup [25 g])
- Cilantro (½ a bunch)
- Garlic cloves (1 bulb)
- Fresh basil (½ a package)
- Fresh dill (¼ of a package)
- Flat leaf parsley (½ a bunch)

NUTS/SEEDS

- Walnut pieces (¼ cup [30 g])
- Sunflower seeds (3 tbsp [27 g])
- Pumpkin seeds (2 tbsp [18 g]), optional
- Cashews (1¼ cups [180 g])
- Pine nuts (4 tbsp [65 g])
- Dry roasted peanuts or sub cashews (¼ cup [37 g])
- Tahini (3 tbsp [45 g])

LEGUMES

- Extra-firm tofu (1 lb [455 g])
- Tempeh (one 8-oz [225-g] package)
- Black beans (½ a 15-oz [425-g] can)
- Kidney beans, optional (⅓ a 15-oz [425-g] can)
- Chickpeas (¼ cup [50 g])
- Cannellini beans (⅓ a 15-oz [425-g] can)
- Dried split peas (1 cup [200 g])
- Frozen shelled edamame (1 cup [155 g])
- Vegan "meatballs," optional

DRESSINGS/SAUCES/EXTRAS

- Taco seasoning
- Smoke sea salt, optional
- Avocado dressing store-bought or add avocado + (½) lemon
- Peanut sauce store-bought or add fresh ginger (2 tbsp [30 g], grated)
- Curry sauce store-bought or add coconut milk (½ cup [120 ml]) + vegetable stock (½ cup [120 ml])

PREP DAY

- Cook quinoa
- Chop vegetables for salads and soups

PERFECT PEAR *Smoothie*

This satisfying green smoothie is the perfect balance of green vegetables, fruit and super seeds. Aiding digestion and giving you slow-release energy, this smoothie will keep you going until lunch. Interestingly, the skin of the pear contains even more fiber and phytonutrients than the flesh, so leave the skin on for extra defense against inflammation in the body.

Servings: 1 | **Prep time:** 5 minutes | **Creation time:** 5 minutes

12 oz (355 ml) vegan milk of choice

½ **a frozen banana**

1 large pear, or 2 small ones, cored

½ **a cucumber**

1 handful of baby spinach

1 heaping tbsp (15 g) flax meal

1 heaping tbsp (15 g) hemp seeds

Stevia to taste, optional

Combine all the ingredients in a high-speed blender and process until smooth. Add more milk if it is too thick.

COCO-NANA *Smoothie*

Rich in flavor and creamy in texture, this awesome smoothie is full of electrolytes, calcium, potassium, good fats and many other essential nutrients. The coconut is both hydrating and satisfying, and will set your day off right. Some stores, such as Whole Foods, carry packaged fresh coconut meat. Otherwise you can choose between buying a whole coconut and preparing it yourself on prep day, or using unsweetened coconut flakes instead.

Servings: 1 | **Prep time:** 2 minutes (does not include time to prepare coconut meat) | **Creation time:** 2 minutes

---

1½–2 cups (355–475 ml) coconut-almond milk or vegan milk of choice

½ tbsp (7 g) raw cacao or substitute Dutch-processed cocoa powder

1 large frozen banana

½ cup (40 g) coconut meat or substitute coconut flakes

1 heaping tbsp (15 g) flax meal

Stevia to taste, optional

Combine all the ingredients in a high-speed blender and process until smooth.

BEET THIS! *Smoothie*

Garnish this brilliantly bright smoothie with an orange slice and spinach leaf and it will be an Instagram hit! Not only is the color beautiful, the taste is out of this world and the nutrient content is through the roof. This is a breakfast that will give you some pep in your step all morning. Beets can stain your hands, so when you peel them, make sure to either wear gloves or wash your hands right away after handling them.

Servings: 1 | **Prep time:** 10 minutes | **Creation time:** 2 minutes

1 beet, peeled

1 orange, peeled and deseeded

1 apple, cored

5 frozen strawberries

1 small handful of baby spinach

½ a banana

2 tbsp (30 g) hemp seeds

½–¾ cup (120–175 ml) water

½" (1.3 cm) slice fresh ginger root to taste, optional

Combine all the ingredients in a high-speed blender and process until smooth.

WARRIOR-WORTHY *Smoothie*

This hearty smoothie is packed full of vitamins and also contains omega-3 fatty acids, so your body, especially your heart, will love you for drinking it! It's loaded with fiber and will improve your digestion, speed up weight loss, as well as lower your cholesterol. Maca powder, made from the Incan super food maca root, is great for aiding in fighting stress, increasing stamina and boosting libido. Therefore, even though it's an optional add-on, it's something you don't want to miss out on!

Servings: 1 | **Prep time:** 5 minutes | **Creation time:** 2 minutes

1 cup (235 ml) vegan milk of choice	Combine all the ingredients in a high-speed blender and process until smooth.
1 kale leaf, stem removed	
1 small handful spinach	
½ an avocado	
4 pitted Medjool dates	
½ a frozen banana	
½ tsp cinnamon	
1 tbsp (15 g) raw maca powder, optional	

BLUEBERRY BONANZA *Smoothie*

High in antioxidants and omega fatty acids, this refreshing smoothie will give you a colorful and delicious jumpstart to the day. As an added bonus, it's also great for hair and skin health. Blueberries have been linked to improving short-term memory; so don't forget to try out this smoothie!

Servings: 1 | **Prep time:** 2 minutes | **Creation time:** 2 minutes

1½ cups (225 g) frozen blueberries or fresh blueberries + 1 ice cube	Combine all the ingredients in a high-speed blender and process until smooth, adding more coconut water if needed to reach the desired thickness.
1 heaping tbsp (15 g) chia seeds	
½ a frozen banana	
½ cup (120 ml) coconut water	
¾ cup (175 ml) vegan milk of choice	
Stevia to taste, optional	
½–1 scoop protein powder, optional	

APPLE ABS OF STEEL *Oatmeal Bowl*

For a hearty start to the day this oatmeal will provide you with long-lasting energy. It's especially good to eat on jog-day, as the buckwheat and walnuts aid the cardiovascular system immensely. You'll also be provided with enough fiber to encourage healthy digestion. Raisins are linked to promoting good intestinal health, speeding up your system and promoting a faster metabolism. Long used in Chinese medicine, goji berries are said to have a positive impact on overall health and organ functioning.

Servings: 2 | **Prep time:** 5 minutes | **Creation time:** 15–20 minutes

1 apple, cored and chopped into bite-size pieces

½ cup (80 g) rolled oats or use steel cut oats, which have a longer cook time

¼ cup (170 g) buckwheat groats or sub more rolled oats

1 cup (235 ml) water

½ cup (120 ml) vegan milk of choice

¼ cup (35 g) raisins

½ tsp cinnamon, or to taste

¼ cup (30 g) walnut pieces

2 tbsp (30 g) coconut flakes

1 heaping tbsp (15 g) hemp seeds

2 tbsp (30 g) goji berries

Stevia to taste

1 tbsp (15 ml) pure maple syrup, optional

Combine the apple, oats, buckwheat, water, milk, raisins and cinnamon in a saucepan over medium-high heat, stirring occasionally.

When it reaches a boil, reduce the heat and simmer until it's thick, about 10 minutes, adding more milk if it becomes too thick.

Once the cereal has reached the desired thickness, add the walnuts, coconut, hemp, goji berries, stevia and optional maple syrup. Stir until thoroughly combined.

You can add a few more walnut pieces, coconut flakes and goji berries on top for a nice presentation.

SOUTHWEST TOFU *Scramble*

High in protein, nutritionally dense and tongue teasingly delicious, you'll be scrambling for a fork once you get this dish out of the pan! Be brave with the hot sauce if you dare, chilies are revered historically for their health promoting properties and capsicum (aka peppers) are said to reduce cravings and promote controlled weight loss. This spicy little number goes perfectly with freshly squeezed grapefruit juice.

Servings: 2 | **Prep time:** 10–15 minutes (does not include pressing the tofu) | **Creation time:** 15–20 minutes

SPICE MIX

¼ tsp turmeric

½ tsp cumin

½ tsp paprika

½ tsp sea salt

Splash of water

1 tbsp (15 ml) grape seed oil

½ a yellow onion, diced

2–3 garlic cloves, minced

½ lb (225 g) extra-firm tofu, drained and pressed*

2 cups (130 g) sliced white mushrooms or mushrooms of choice

¾ cup (115 g) diced red bell pepper or bell pepper of choice—or use a precut frozen mix

Diced jalapeño to taste, optional

½ cup (85 g) cooked black beans, canned beans are fine

2 cups (60 g) baby spinach, chopped

1 tbsp (15 g) nutritional yeast

Black pepper to taste

Fresh cilantro, optional

Hot sauce to taste, optional

Salsa, optional

In a small bowl, combine the spice mix ingredients, adding the splash of water to make it into a sauce. Set aside.

In a large skillet set to medium-high with grape seed oil, sauté the onion and garlic for a couple of minutes. Crumble the tofu with your hands as you add it to the pan. Next, add the mushrooms to the mixture and continue to saute another 5 minutes. Add the bell pepper and optional jalapeño and continue to sauté for another couple minutes.

Last, add the black beans, spinach, spice mix, nutritional yeast, black pepper and optional cilantro, and mix until thoroughly combined and hot.

Serve with optional salsa and/or hot sauce.

*PRESSING TOFU

Tofu generally comes in a block packed in water to preserve freshness. For most recipes using extra-firm or firm tofu, it's helpful to remove the excess water from the block for a few reasons. The texture will be more desirable in most dishes, it will brown more easily and it will soak up marinades and sauces better. To press tofu, place the block on a small towel or a few layers of paper towels on a plate. Take another small plate or cutting board and place it on top of the tofu, and then find something small and heavy to place on top of that. It's a bit of a balancing act so don't use anything that will break if it falls! Press for at least 15 minutes, but if possible, give it 30 minutes to an hour.

COLOR-ME-BAD CHOPPED Salad

This beautiful salad contains a wide variety of vibrantly colored vegetables. More colors means more different nutrients! Woohoo! The garbanzo beans (aka chickpeas), quinoa and pumpkin seeds enhance the salad with protein and texture. Feel free to adjust the amounts of each vegetable based on your likes and dislikes. The dressing recipe will make two servings, so save half to use on an upcoming salad recipe this week. Buying a premade dressing at the store is always an option as well, just make sure it is clean and free of chemicals and trans fats.

Servings: 1 full meal-size salad and an extra serving of dressing | **Prep time:** 15 minutes (not including cooking quinoa) | **Creation time:** 5 minutes

AVOCADO DRESSING (OR SUB A STORE-BOUGHT VARIATION)

½ an avocado

2 tbsp (30 ml) extra virgin olive oil

1 large lemon, juiced

¾ cup (45 g) fresh flat-leaf parsley

1-2 garlic cloves (or ⅛ tsp garlic powder)

Celtic or Himalayan sea salt

Pepper to taste

3 oz (85 g) chopped romaine and/or mixed greens of choice, about 3 handfuls

¼ cup (35 g) chopped cucumber

¼ cup (28 g) shredded carrot

¼ cup (35 g) chopped red, yellow or orange bell pepper

¼ cup (40 g) chopped tomatoes

½ cup (125 g) canned garbanzo beans, drained, rinsed and patted dry

2 tbsp (18 g) pumpkin and/or sunflower seeds

½ cup (90 g) cooked quinoa*

Combine all dressing ingredients in a blender and process until smooth and creamy. Add water if it's too thick.

Combine all of the salad ingredients in a large bowl. Toss in 2 tablespoons (30 ml) of the dressing you have prepared. Put the rest of the dressing in a small container and save in the fridge for future use. Toss the salad and eat immediately so that it doesn't get soggy.

*COOKING QUINOA

If there are instructions on the package, follow those. If you buy bulk, you are likely to benefit by soaking the quinoa overnight before cooking. Rinse the quinoa after soaking and place 1 cup (185 g) of quinoa with 1 cup (235 ml) of water or vegetable broth in a medium saucepan. Bring to a boil then reduce heat, cover and simmer for about 15 minutes. If the water has not all been absorbed after 20 minutes, drain the excess water from the pot. Allow the quinoa to cool for 5-10 minutes and then "fluff" it with a fork.

TASTE OF MEXICO *Bowl*

Fresh, crunchy and delicious, this salad will perk up your taste buds and fill your bowl with color. The addition of cilantro makes for a detoxifying effect that complements the antioxidant properties of the red onion, yum! This lunch is high in nutrients, satisfaction and taste.

Servings: 1 meal-size salad | **Prep time:** 10–15 minutes | **Creation time:** 10 minutes

¾ cup (190 g) black and/or kidney beans, drained and rinsed

1 tsp taco seasoning

Hot sauce to taste

2 cups (110 g) chopped romaine lettuce

⅓ cup (60 g) diced fresh tomatoes

⅓ cup (40 g) chopped cucumber

⅓ cup (50 g) chopped green bell pepper

1 tbsp (15 g) diced jalapeño, optional

¼ cup (40 g) diced red onion, optional

2 tbsp (30 ml) Avocado Dressing (see page 44)

2 tbsp (30 g) salsa

¼ of an avocado, sliced

3 tbsp (45 g) chopped cilantro

Combine the beans, taco seasoning and hot sauce in a small bowl and set aside.

In a large bowl, toss the lettuce, tomatoes, cucumber, bell pepper, jalapeño and onion with the avocado dressing.

Place the seasoned beans on top of the lettuce mixture, followed by the salsa and avocado slices, and garnish with the cilantro.

ITALIAN CANNELLINI BEAN AND FENNEL *Salad*

On top of having a hint of licorice and anise taste, fennel packs a punch in the antioxidant department as well as being high in vitamin C and essential minerals. You'll get a flavor-fest from the dressing, and the beans will fill you up, keep your energy levels high and your hunger pangs low. Enjoy little pops of caper saltiness with this Italian inspired salad!

Servings: 1-2 | **Prep time:** 10 minutes | **Creation time:** 5-8 minutes

3 oz (85 g) Italian-blend mixed greens, about 3 handfuls

¾ cup (110 g) thinly sliced fennel

½ cup (90 g) chopped tomato

½ tbsp (7 g) capers

¼ cup (25 g) black olives or olives of choice, pitted and sliced

½-1 stalk green onion, chopped

¾ cup (190 g) canned cannellini beans, drained and rinsed

1 tbsp (15 g) chopped fresh basil

Black pepper to taste

DRESSING (OR SUB A STORE-BOUGHT VERSION)

½ a small lemon juiced

⅛ tsp garlic powder or 1 clove garlic, crushed

1 tbsp (15 ml) extra virgin olive oil

½ tbsp Dijon mustard

½ tsp Italian seasoning

⅛ tsp salt

Combine the mixed greens, fennel, tomatoes, capers, olives, green onion and cannellini beans in a large bowl.

In a small bowl, whisk together the dressing ingredients.

Toss some dressing with the portion of the salad you plan to eat immediately. Keep the rest of the dressing and salad separate until you are ready to eat it so it doesn't get too soggy.

Sprinkle with basil and add fresh black pepper to taste.

CAULIFLOWER FOR CUT ABS *Soup*

This cauliflower soup is one of my favorites. It's flavorful, rich and creamy and it's incredibly easy to make! High in antioxidants, this soup will help boost your cardiovascular system, and its substantial thickness will fill you up and help you avoid midnight snacking.

Servings: 4 meal-size portions | **Prep time:** 10–15 minutes (not including soaking the cashews) | **Creation time:** 40 minutes stove top method or 1½–2 hours in the slow cooker + 10 minutes kitchen time to blend

2 cups (475 ml) vegetable broth, low sodium

1 head cauliflower, chopped

1 yellow or white onion, sliced

2 celery stalks, sliced

1 tbsp (15 g) dried chives

4 cloves garlic

¼ tsp sea salt to taste

Pepper to taste

⅔ cup (90 g) cashews, soaked 6–8 hours if using stovetop cooking method

1 tbsp (15 ml) extra virgin olive oil

2+ cups (475+ ml) flax milk or vegan milk of choice

STOVETOP

In a stockpot, bring the vegetable broth, cauliflower, onion, celery, chives, garlic, salt and pepper to a boil.

Reduce heat, cover and simmer until vegetables are tender, about 20 minutes.

Meanwhile, drain and rinse the cashews.

When the vegetables are tender, transfer to your high-speed blender, add the soaked cashews, olive oil and milk, and process until smooth and creamy. Add more milk if it's too thick.

SLOW COOKER

Place all the ingredients except the milk in your slow cooker. If you haven't soaked the cashews, they should go in the slow cooker, too. If you have soaked the cashews, drain and rinse them and put aside—they do not need to cook.

Cook on high for 1½ to 2 hours until all the veggies are tender.

Transfer to your high-speed blender, add milk and cashews (if they were soaked) and process until smooth and creamy. Add more milk if necessary to reach the desired thickness.

Easy LIMA BEANS

Easy lima beans are great paired with Cauliflower Soup (page 48), or any dish, to bring some high protein, fibrous legumes to the table with minimal effort.

Servings: 2 | **Prep time:** 5 minutes | **Creation time:** 10 minutes

¾ cup (175 ml) vegetable broth, or sub water

1 cup (120 g) frozen lima beans

1 tsp (15 ml) olive oil (healthier) or vegan buttery spread

Herbamare seasoning, or sub sea salt, to taste

Black pepper to taste

Bring broth to a boil in a saucepan. Add lima beans, bring back to a boil, lower heat and simmer for 5 to 7 minutes until the beans are tender. Remove from heat, drain, put in a bowl and add olive oil or vegan spread and Herbamare or salt and pepper to taste.

COOL CUCUMBER DILL *Soup* & QUINOA WITH SWEET GREEN PEAS

This recipe will definitely make the top of your list for the simplest, most delightful soup possible! If being incredibly delicious isn't enough, dill is known to aid digestion and boost the immune system. Pair it with the refreshingly cool taste of cucumber and you've got yourself a match made in heaven! It's easy enough to make a single serving, but tasty enough to want leftovers, so double the recipe if you want to plan on eating it again this week!

Paired with the soup is a quick and easy quinoa side dish. Quinoa has double the protein of rice and contains all nine essential amino acids. Coupled with sweet peas and fresh pops of parsley, this side will leave your belly full and your mouth smiling. Lightly toasting the sunflower seeds adds an extra crunch!

COOL CUCUMBER DILL SOUP

Servings: 1 large lunch-size portion | **Prep time:** 5 minutes | **Creation time:** 5 minutes + 30 minutes to chill in fridge

1 medium English cucumber 1 stalk green onion ½ a small avocado, pitted ½ cup (32 g) loosely packed fresh dill ¼ tsp Himalayan or Celtic sea salt ¼ of a fresh lemon, deseeded and juiced ½–1 cup (120–235 ml) plain, unsweetened nut milk of choice	Combine all the ingredients in a high-speed blender. Start with ½ cup (120 ml) milk and add more if needed to reach desired thickness. Blend until smooth, and chill 30 minutes before serving.

QUINOA WITH SWEET GREEN PEAS

Servings: 1 | **Prep time:** 5 minutes (not including cooking the quinoa) | **Creation time:** 10 minutes

½ cup (65 g) frozen green peas 1 tbsp (9 g) sunflower seeds ½ cup (90 g) cooked quinoa 1 tbsp (4 g) fresh chopped flat leaf parsley, or 1 tsp dried ½ tbsp (7 g) coconut oil (healthier) or vegan buttery spread Sea salt to taste Cracked black pepper to taste	Bring a small saucepan filled halfway with water to boil. Add the frozen peas and bring back to boiling. Meanwhile, lightly toast the sunflower seeds in the toaster oven—this is optional but recommended. Reduce heat slightly and cook at a rolling boil until peas are tender, about 5 minutes. Drain the peas in a colander and return to pot. Add the rest of the ingredients and stir constantly over medium heat until thoroughly combined and heated, about 5 minutes.

SEDUCTIVE SPLIT PEA *Soup* & STOVETOP TOMATOES

This slow cooker soup is full of flavors that have had time to mix and mature, leaving you with a deeply filling meal, wrapped in extra aromas from the spices. The fiber will boost your digestion and the big dose of carrots will give you lots of vitamin A, keeping your skin glowing. I have really grown to love slow cookers recently. They are a great kitchen tool because they do all the work for you! Throw everything in, blow a kiss goodnight and wake up to a prepared meal, ready to serve when you get home for dinner. Quick-cooking, Italian-herbed cherry tomatoes make a great side to complete the meal.

SEDUCTIVE SPLIT PEA & CARROT SOUP

Servings: 3–4 meal-size portions | **Prep time:** 15 minutes | **Creation time:** 5 minutes kitchen time + 12 hours in the slow cooker

1 cup (195 g) dried split peas

5 cups (1.2 L) vegetable stock

1 tbsp (15 ml) extra virgin olive oil, optional

2 cloves garlic, chopped

1 small yellow onion, peeled and diced

2½ cups (325 g) chopped carrots

2 stalks celery, diced

1 large handful spinach

¼ tsp black pepper

1 tsp dried thyme

½ tsp onion powder

1 tsp cumin

1 tsp curry powder

1 bay leaf

1 tsp sea salt to taste

Pinch of turmeric, optional

1 tbsp (15 ml) red wine, optional

Rinse the split peas.

Combine all the ingredients in the slow cooker and mix well.

Cook on low for around 12 hours.

Remove the bay leaf and use an immersion blender to process the soup for a thicker, purée-style soup—my recommendation. You also have the option to eat it unblended if you prefer a chunky soup.

STOVETOP TOMATOES

Servings: 2 side portions | **Prep time:** 2 minutes | **Creation time:** 8–10 minutes

½ tbsp (7 ml) extra virgin olive oil

2 cups (300 g) cherry tomatoes, chopped in half

1 tsp Italian seasoning

Couple dashes of garlic powder, to taste

Sea salt to taste

Black pepper to taste

Heat a frying pan to medium/medium-low and add the extra virgin olive oil.

Place the tomatoes in the pan and cook for a couple minutes, stirring occasionally so they don't stick to the pan.

Add the Italian seasoning, garlic powder, salt and pepper.

Sauté for 5 to 10 minutes until the tomatoes reach a tenderness that appeals to you.

CURRY ME HOME & VEG Stir Fry

Ready to chill at home after a long day's work? You can quickly fill your kitchen with delicious smells and your body with a tasty cocktail of vegetables, legumes and nuts with this tofu stir fry. You'll find a variety of textures, from soft to chewy to crunchy to mix things up, along with the flavorful kick of curry. Nutritionally, this dish is dense in protein, vitamins and minerals, yet light in calories. Perfect for dropping body fat the healthy way!

Servings: 2 | **Prep time:** 10–15 minutes or less if you use precut vegetables (does not include pressing the tofu) | **Creation time:** 15 minutes

1 tsp coconut oil

2 garlic cloves, minced

½ block of extra-firm tofu, drained, pressed* and cut into ½" (1.3 cm) cubes

VEGETABLES (OR USE PRECUT FROZEN STIR-FRY VEGETABLE MIX)

½ a zucchini, sliced

½ a yellow squash, sliced

1 cup (90 g) chopped baby bok choy (or regular bok choy), stems and leaves separated

½ a red bell pepper, sliced

⅓ cup (50 g) snow peas, destemmed

⅓ cup (50 g) baby corn

SAUCE (OR USE STORE-BOUGHT VERSION)

½ cup (120 ml) coconut milk

½ cup (120 ml) vegetable stock

½ tbsp (7 g) curry powder

½ tsp garlic powder

½ tbsp (7 g) cornstarch

Few dashes of red pepper flakes to taste, optional

Sea salt and black pepper to taste

¼ cup (35 g) cashew halves

Heat a sauté pan with coconut oil to medium-high heat. Add the garlic and sauté for about 30 seconds.

Place the tofu cubes, zucchini and squash in the pan and sauté. When the zucchini and squash begin to tenderize, about 4 minutes, add the stems of the bok choy and red pepper. Last, add the snow peas, leafy part of the bok choy and baby corn.

Meanwhile, whisk together the sauce ingredients in a bowl.

Once the sauté mix starts to get tender, about 6 to 8 minutes, reduce the heat to medium and push the vegetables toward the outside edges of the pan.

Pour the sauce in the middle and stir so it doesn't stick to the pan. Once it thickens, mix it into the tofu and vegetables until thoroughly combined.

Toast the cashew halves in the toaster oven until they are slightly browned. Add the cashews to the stir fry and enjoy.

*For instructions on pressing tofu see page 43.

MUAY THAI ZUCCHINI *Noodles*

Unleash your inner warrior with this kickin' low carb meal for lunch or dinner any day of the week. It's a perfect opportunity to have some fun with your spiralizer to create a flavorful, fat-fighting meal. By using zucchini instead of pasta, you eliminate grains from the meal completely and still get the feel of eating noodles. The Thai peanut sauce is rich and satisfying and the edamame adds a ton of complete protein to the meal.

Servings: 2 | **Prep time:** 15–20 minutes | **Creation time:** 5 minutes

---

1 cup (155 g) frozen shelled edamame

2 large zucchini, spiralized, or julienned if you don't have a spiralizer

2 large summer squash, spiralized

1 red bell pepper, deseeded and finely sliced or julienned

1 large carrot, shredded

¼ cup (35 g) dry roasted peanuts or sub cashews

1 tbsp (8 g) black sesame seeds

SAUCE (OR USE A STORE-BOUGHT VERSION)

2–4 tbsp (30–60 ml) vegetable broth (salt free)

4 tbsp (65 g) natural peanut butter or sub almond butter

2 tbsp (30 ml) Bragg Liquid Aminos or sub tamari

1 garlic clove, minced or sub ⅛ tsp garlic powder

2–4 tsp (10–20 ml) hot sauce (depending on how spicy you like it)

2 tsp (10 ml) sesame oil

2 tsp (10 g) fresh-grated ginger or sub ½ tsp ground ginger

2 tbsp (30 ml) apple cider vinegar

Black pepper to taste

Bring a medium-size pot of water to a boil. Add the edamame and cook for about 5 minutes until they become slightly tender. Drain.

Place the zucchini and squash "noodles," red bell pepper and carrots on a paper towel and pat dry.

In a small bowl, whisk together all the sauce ingredients. Start with just 2 tablespoons (30 ml) of vegetable broth and add more if you prefer a thinner sauce.

In a large bowl, combine the zucchini, squash, bell pepper, carrots and edamame.

Add the sauce and toss.

Place a portion in a bowl or on a plate and then sprinkle with the peanuts, sesame seeds and black pepper on top.

Serve immediately or it will get soggy. Enjoy!

TAHINI-TOPPED ROASTED CAULIFLOWER *florets* & GRILLED TEMPEH

This is one of my favorite dishes because of how rich and satisfying it is. The cauliflower is actually so filling I often eat it as my entire main course and you are welcome to do the same! The meal is also very low in carbs and easy to prepare—what more could you ask for? Take note that when you are creating the sauce, it will thicken when you heat it, so don't worry if it seems too thin at first. The tahini sauce doubles as sauce for the tempeh as well!

Speaking of tempeh, whether you're after a quick, healthy snack full of flavor and bite, or just an accompaniment to a meal, grilled tempeh is a great choice. With higher amounts of protein and dietary fiber, as well as a higher vitamin content than tofu, this simple recipe packs a big punch for your health as well as your taste buds!

TAHINI-TOPPED ROASTED CAULIFLOWER FLORETS

Servings: 2 large portions | **Prep time:** 10–15 minutes | **Creation time:** 30 minutes

1 large head of cauliflower, cut into 1" (2.5 cm) florets

1 tbsp (15 ml) extra virgin olive oil, divided

3 tbsp (45 g) tahini

4 tbsp (60 ml) fresh lemon juice

4 tbsp (60 ml) apple cider vinegar

¼ tsp sea salt

¼–½ cup (60–120 ml) water

2 cloves garlic, minced

1 tbsp (8 g) white sesame seeds

2 tbsp (8 g) finely chopped flat-leaf parsley (or 1 tsp dried)

Preheat oven to 450°F (230°C) with the rack in the top position.

Cut and divide the head of cauliflower into 1–1½-inch (2.5–3.8-cm) florets. Toss the cauliflower with 2 teaspoons (10 ml) olive oil, and then bake for approximately 20 minutes. It should prove tender using the fork test and appear slightly brown.

Meanwhile, in a small bowl, whisk together the tahini, lemon juice, cider vinegar, salt and water.

In a saucepan, heat the remaining 1 teaspoon (5 ml) of olive oil to medium heat. Add the garlic and sauté for 1 to 2 minutes until it starts to brown.

Turn the heat to low and add the sauce, stirring thoroughly as it thickens for about a minute. Remove the pan from the heat.

Serve the cauliflower onto your plate, pour sauce over the florets and sprinkle the sesame seeds and parsley on top.

GRILLED TEMPEH

Servings: 4 side portions | **Prep time:** 15 minutes (including 10 minutes of letting the spices absorb into the tempeh) |
Creation time: 10 minutes

1 package of tempeh*

1 tbsp (15 ml) sesame oil

SPICE RUB (OR USE A SIMILAR
STORE-BOUGHT SPICE MIX)

½ tsp garlic powder

½ tsp onion powder

½ tsp dry mustard powder

**¼ tsp smoked paprika or regular
paprika**

⅛ tsp black pepper

¼ tsp dried oregano

¼ tsp dried thyme

**⅛ tsp smoked sea salt or regular
sea salt**

Dash of red pepper flakes to taste

Remove the tempeh from package and cut it into slices no more than ½ inch (1.3 cm) thick.

Combine the spice rub ingredients in a small bowl.

Gently rub the spice mix into the tempeh slices and let stand for at least 10 minutes. Save the leftover spice rub to use as a seasoning salt for other dishes.

Heat a frying pan with sesame oil to medium-high. Place the tempeh slices in the pan and cook 4 to 5 minutes on one side until it has browned, then flip and brown the other side.

*For convenience, you can also buy tempeh that is already cooked and flavored. Simply heat and serve according to the directions on the package.

STEAMY SPAGHETTI SQUASH *Marinara*

For a brightly colored meal filled with omega-3 and omega-6 fatty acids—which are great for the heart and brain and even promote weight loss—look no further! I have my dad to thank for introducing me to this awesome vegetable countless years ago. In this particular recipe, we top the squash with marinara sauce and rich pine nuts to give your senses a field day! Did you know squash could be this much fun to eat?

Servings: 1–2 | **Prep time:** 8–10 minutes | **Creation time:** 40–45 minutes

1 small spaghetti squash

1½ cups (355 ml) marinara sauce to taste

Vegan meatballs,* optional

3 tbsp (45 g) pine nuts

Nutritional yeast to taste, optional

Sea salt and pepper to taste

Preheat oven to 450°F (232°C).

Cut spaghetti squash in half and scrape out the seeds. Place the two halves cut side down in a dish or oven tray lined with foil.

Bake for 30 to 40 minutes, depending on the size of the squash, until fully cooked. Your fork should be able to penetrate the skin but still meet some resistance.

Once the spaghetti squash is done, remove it from oven, flip the halves over and let them cool enough for you to handle.

Meanwhile, heat the marinara sauce in a small saucepan or in the microwave. If you choose to add vegan meatballs, cook them according to the directions.

Using a large fork, scrape out the squash strands into a bowl. Add the marinara sauce and optional meatballs.

Sprinkle with pine nuts and optional nutritional yeast for a "cheesy" flavor addition. Add sea salt and black pepper to taste.

*Brand suggestions: 365, Amy's, Gardein, Nate's

CHIA-OCOLATE Pudding

This completely guilt-free dessert will not only cure your chocolate craving in an instant, but also flood your body with super nutrients such as omega-3 fatty acids and antioxidants. The chia seeds give it that pudding consistency and by blending them thoroughly, you won't even notice them! Who says we can't have chocolate on a healthy diet?

Servings: 2 | **Prep time:** 2 minutes | **Creation time:** 5 minutes + 2 hours to chill

1½ cups (355 ml) vegan milk of choice

¼ cup (35 g) chia seeds

4 Medjool dates, pitted

⅓ of a banana

2 tbsp (30 g) raw unsweetened cacao powder

½ tsp pure vanilla extract

⅛ tsp sea salt

Stevia powder to taste, optional

1 tbsp (15 g) unsweetened coconut flakes, for garnish

Combine all the ingredients except the stevia and coconut flakes in your high-speed blender. Blend until completely smooth, like pudding.

Taste. If it's not sweet enough for you, add a dash of stevia powder. Blend again and repeat if necessary. It's important not to add too much or it will become bitter.

Chill for 2 hours before serving.

Garnish individual servings by sprinkling coconut flakes on top.

CRAZY FOR COCONUT *Bites*

There's no way you will be missing junk food while eating this sweet treat! Quick and easy to create, there's no cooking involved. These dessert balls can be stored in the fridge or freezer—just make sure you protect them from freezer burn by keeping them in a suitable bag—but I can't imagine there will be leftovers for long, especially if you are not the only one in the house. This is a great one to share.

Servings: 2 | **Prep time:** 30 minutes to soak the dates | **Creation time:** 10-15 min

¼ **cup (36 g) cashews pieces**

6 Medjool dates, pitted and soaked 30 minutes

1 tsp vanilla extract

1 tsp pure maple syrup

¼ **cup (20 g) coconut flakes**

Process the cashews in a food processor until they are ground into tiny pieces—you can also put them in a baggie and crush them with the rounded side of a big spoon. Remove from the processor or baggie and set aside.

Combine the dates, vanilla and maple syrup in food processor and blend until the mixture has turned into a paste—it doesn't have to be perfectly blended.

Add cashew pieces and coconut flakes and blend until you can form the mixture into small balls with your hands.

Chill in the freezer for 15 minutes before eating.

Store in a sealed container in the fridge or freezer.

WEEK 2

OVERVIEW

	MON	TUES	WED	THURS	FRI	SAT	SUN
BREAKFAST	Orange-sicle Smoothie	Chocolate Brazil Booty Smoothie	Basil Strawberryita Smoothie	Banana Bread Smoothie	Awesome Acai Smoothie	Pineapple Power Parfait	Avocado-Topped BLT & Homemade Brazil Nut Milk
LUNCH	Mindful Mediterranean Salad	Luscious Leftovers	Scrumptious Spinach Seed Salad	Luscious Leftovers	Smoked Egg-less Egg Salad	Luscious Leftovers	
SNACK	Fresh Fruit of Choice	Fresh Fruit of Choice	Fresh Fruit of Choice	Fresh Fruit of Choice	Fresh Fruit of Choice	Fresh Fruit of Choice	Fresh Fruit of Choice
DINNER	Two Bean Protein Chili with Sliced Avocado	Wasabi Cauliflower Mash & Easy Broccoli	Bella Broccoli Soup & Quinoa Side	Asian Tofu with Snow Peas & Bamboo Shoots	Warm Me Up White Bean Soup & Steamed Zucchini Halves	Muscle-Building Mung Bean Fettuccini Alfredo	Fiesta Pizza
TREAT	X	X	Decadent Chocolate-Raspberry Mousse	X	X	X	Pining for Pineapple Frozen Dessert
WORKOUT	Cross-Train (full body focus)	Cardio + Yoga	Cross-Train (upper body focus)	Cardio	Cross-Train (lower body focus)	Yoga + Cardio	Off/Rest

GROCERY LIST - WEEK 2

LIQUIDS

- Coconut water (12 oz [355 ml])
- Vegan milk of choice (48 oz [1.4 L])
- Vegetable broth (64 oz [1.9 L])

FRUIT

- Avocados (2)
- Bananas (4)
- Lemon (1–2)
- Oranges, mandarin/seedless (4–5)
- Pineapple chunks (1 cup [150 g])
- Frozen acai fruit (1 cup [165 g])
- Frozen blueberries (½ cup [75 g])
- Frozen mango (½ cup [75 g])
- Frozen raspberries (½ cup [125 g])
- Frozen strawberries (1½ cups [380 g])
- Dates, Medjool (13)
- Golden raisins (2 tbsp [30 g])

LEAFY GREENS

- Baby spinach (5 handfuls)
- Romaine lettuce (9 cups [500 g] chopped)

VEGETABLES

- Bell pepper, green (½)
- Bell pepper, red (½)
- Broccoli florets (4–5 cups [285–355 g])
- Cauliflower (2 heads)
- Cucumber (½–1)
- Jalapeño (¼–½) optional
- Mushrooms (½ an 8-oz [115-g] package)
- Onion, green (1 stalk)
- Onion, red (½)
- Onion, yellow (2)
- Snow peas (1½ cups [275 g])
- Tomato (1)

- Zucchini (1)
- Frozen broccoli florets (2 cups [315 g])
- Frozen green peas (1 cup [130 g])
- Bamboo shoots, canned (¾ cup [55 g])
- Diced tomatoes (one 14.5-oz [410-g] can)
- Tomato paste (one 6-oz [170-g] can)
- Fresh basil (¼ oz [7 g])
- Fresh cilantro (½ cup [8 g])
- Fresh dill (2–3 sprigs)
- Fresh parsley, (5 tbsp [20 g] chopped)
- Fresh rosemary (½ a sprig) or sub dried
- Garlic (1 bulb)

NUTS/SEEDS

- Almond slivers, cashews or pine nuts (3 tbsp [45 g])
- Brazil nuts (1½ cups [210 g])
- Cashews (1 cup [145 g])
- Pecan pieces (2 tbsp [30 g])
- Pumpkin seeds (2 tbsp [18 g])
- Sunflower seeds (¼ cup [37 g])
- Walnuts (¾ cup [90 g])

LEGUMES

- Explore Asian Edamame & Mung Bean fettuccini (½ a package)
- Tempeh bacon (3 strips)
- Tofu, extra-firm (1 lb [455 g])
- Textured vegetable protein (TVP) (½ cup [45 g])
- Vegan beef crumbles (optional)
- Black beans (¼ of a 15-oz [425-g] can)
- Cannellini beans (two 15-oz [425-g] cans)
- Chickpeas (⅓ of a 15-oz [425-g] can)
- Kidney beans (one 15-oz [425-g] can)
- Pinto beans (one 15-oz [425-g] can)

VEGAN DAIRY

- Daiya mozzarella to taste
- Vegan yogurt (2½ cups [575 g])

WHOLE GRAIN

- Whole grain English muffin or sub 2 slices toast, sprouted if available
- Whole grain tortilla, sprouted if available

DRESSINGS/SAUCES/EXTRAS

- Artichoke hearts (¼ cup [75 g])
- Black olives (½ cup [50 g])
- Pizza sauce (1 cup [235 ml])
- Wasabi powder
- Smoked seasoning salt, optional
- Tahini dressing, optional
- Poppy seed dressing, store-bought version or add poppy seeds (2 tsp [10 g]) + dates (2)

PREP DAY

- Cook quinoa
- Chop vegetables for salads and soups
- Steam cauliflower
- Press tofu

CHOCOLATE BRAZIL BOOTY *Smoothie*

Nutty and rich, this incredible smoothie gives you motivation to wake up in the morning. In addition to the fantastic Brazil nut flavor, it has a kick of cacao, one of the raw healthy super foods. Start your day knowing that you can simultaneously nourish your body, get your metabolism rolling and cure a chocolate craving.

Servings: 1 | **Prep time:** 2 minutes | **Creation time:** 5 minutes

8–10 oz (235–285 ml) coconut water

4 oz (120 ml) vegan nut milk of choice

1 large or 2 small frozen bananas

8 Brazil nuts

1 tbsp (15 g) raw cacao

½–1 scoop protein powder

Stevia powder to taste

Combine all the ingredients in a high-speed blender and process until smooth.

BANANA BREAD *Smoothie*

Reminiscent of tasty banana bread, this filling smoothie is packed with goodness. Include protein powder for added amino acids if you like. Either way, you will be taking in tons of essential nutrients. This smoothie will not only leave you feeling completely satisfied, but it's also great for improving digestion.

Servings: 1 | **Prep time:** 5 minutes | **Creation time:** 2 minutes

1½ cups (355 ml) vegan milk of choice

5 dates, pitted

½ cup (60 g) walnuts

1 large frozen banana

1 tsp vanilla extract

½–1 scoop vegan protein powder, optional

Cinnamon to taste

½ cup (40 g) rolled oats

Combine all the ingredients in a high-speed blender and process until smooth.

ORANGE-SICLE *Smoothie*

This super smoothie reminds me of the frozen orange pops I used to eat as a kid, only these have a big boost of vitamin C to get that fat burning kick-started without any processed sugars! Amla powder is an incredible addition because it has a higher concentration of antioxidants than any other food, even berries! The hemp seeds offer protein, but if you are looking to build muscle quickly, throw in some protein powder as well.

Servings: 1 | **Prep time:** 5 minutes | **Creation time:** 2 minutes

2-3 oranges of choice, deseeded and peeled	Combine all the ingredients in a high-speed blender and process until smooth and creamy.
1½-2 cups (355-475 ml) vegan milk of choice	
1 large frozen banana	
2 tbsp (30 g) hemp seeds	
1 tbsp (15 g) flax meal	
1 tsp amla powder, optional	
½-1 scoop plain or vanilla vegan protein powder, optional	

AWESOME ACAI *Smoothie*

Sweet and tart, this mouthwatering smoothie is a fantastic option for breakfast. The acai fruit is rich in antioxidants and is known to have many beneficial disease-fighting properties. The coconut water hydrates your body, helping you stay energized and detoxified and reduces unwanted water weight. It's a nutrient-filled treat that will keep you strong and ready for whatever comes next in your day.

Servings: 1 | **Prep time:** 5 minutes | **Creation time:** 2 minutes

1 cup (145 g) frozen acai fruit	Combine all the ingredients in a high-speed blender and process until smooth.
½ cup (75 g) frozen blueberries	
¾-1 cup (175-235 ml) coconut water	
½ cup (115 g) vegan yogurt, plain/unsweetened, or sub ¼ cup (60 ml) vegan milk	
1-2 tbsp (30-60 g) flax meal	
Banana, optional	

BASIL STRAWBERRYITA *Smoothie*

The strawberry-basil combination in this recipe is both gorgeous to look at and refreshing to drink. Basil is well known for having remarkable wholesome benefits from curtailing stress to freshening up skin. Begin the morning with a little less tension and a little more brightness! The banana will also help sustain you until lunch while boosting your potassium levels.

Servings: 1 | **Prep time:** 5 minutes | **Creation time:** 2 minutes

---

4 large basil leaves

1 small handful baby spinach

½ cup (120 ml) vegan milk of choice

1 cup (235 ml) coconut water

1½ cups (380 g) frozen strawberries

1 frozen banana, or substitute a fresh banana

1 tbsp (15 g) hemp seeds

Stevia powder to taste, optional

1 tbsp (15 g) raw maca powder, recommended, optional

Combine all the ingredients in a high-speed blender and process until smooth.

PINEAPPLE POWER Parfait

This badass meal is colorful, sweet and filled with interesting textures. Your bowl will be brimming with omega-3 fatty acids, vitamin C and healthy nut proteins. Pineapple is especially great for helping us achieve fitness goals by reducing inflammation and joint pain and improving circulation, heart and bone health. This breakfast aids in speeding up your body's ability to burn fat and fuel your day.

Servings: 1 | **Prep time:** 5 minutes if pineapple is precut, 10 minutes if you start with a whole pineapple | **Creation time:** 5 minutes

1 cup (230 g) vegan yogurt, unsweetened and/or plain flavored*

1 cup (165 g) fresh pineapple chunks

2 tbsp (30 g) hemp seeds

2 tbsp (30 g) walnut pieces

2 tbsp (30 g) pecan pieces

2 tbsp (30 g) coconut flakes

½ cup (75 g) fresh blueberries, optional

2–4 tbsp (30–60 g) fruit sweetened granola, optional

Place all ingredients in your bowl in the order listed and enjoy!

*Recommended brand: So Delicious Cultured Coconut Milk

AVOCADO-TOPPED BLT & HOMEMADE BRAZIL NUT Milk

This brunch is a healthy take on the popular classic BLT sandwich. You'll start your day full of fight, with lasting energy and a jump-started metabolism to speed up that weight loss. Enjoy your sandwich with a side of fresh, selenium-rich, creamy Brazil nut milk.

Once the package is opened, tempeh will not stay fresh for long, so I recommend you go ahead and cook the entire package, and use some for leftovers during the upcoming week.

AVOCADO-TOPPED BLT

Servings: 1 | **Prep time:** 5 minutes | **Creation time:** 15 minutes

2-4 strips of vegan tempeh bacon,* cut in half or thirds to fit in your English muffin

1 sprouted whole grain English muffin, or sub 2 slices sprouted whole grain bread

½ tbsp (7 g) vegan buttery spread, optional

1 tbsp (15 g) vegan mayonnaise

1-2 large tomato slices

1 romaine lettuce leaf

3-4 avocado slices, optional

Cook the tempeh bacon according to the directions on the package.

Split the English muffin in half. Spread a thin layer of buttery spread on each slice (optional) and toast.

Once toasted, spread the vegan mayo on the top slice.

Place the tempeh on the other slice, followed by tomato slices, folded lettuce, optional avocado slices and then the top of the English muffin.

*Brand suggestion: Lightlife Fakin' Bacon

HOMEMADE BRAZIL NUT MILK

Servings: 2 | **Prep time:** 12 hours of soaking the nuts | **Creation time:** 15 minutes

1 cup (145 g) raw Brazil nuts, soaked 12+ hours

3–3½ cups (410–530 ml) water—depending how thick you like it

3 Medjool dates, pitted, soaking 30+ minutes is recommended but not required

1 tsp pure vanilla extract

½ tsp cinnamon to taste

After soaking the Brazil nuts at least 12 hours, drain and rinse them.

Place all the ingredients in a high-speed blender and work the speed up to high and blend thoroughly until fully liquidated.

Pour the contents into a nut milk bag that you have placed in a large bowl in the sink. Slowly, strain the liquid through the bag by twisting and squeezing it until no more liquid will come out.

Pour a serving into your glass, and keep the rest in a tightly sealed container in the fridge. It's best if you consume it within 2 days, but it will last for about 3 days.

SCRUMPTIOUS SPINACH SEED *Salad*

Wow! Yum! Crunch! This easily assembled salad certainly brightens up your plate. With high levels of vitamin K and A, plus huge amounts of manganese and folate, your body will be happy and you'll enjoy long-lasting satisfaction from all of the seeds. Just make sure to have floss handy for the little seeds that like to take shelter between your teeth!

Servings: 1 meal-size salad + an extra serving of dressing to save | **Prep time:** 5–10 minutes (+ 30 minutes to soak the dates if you go with that option) | **Creation time:** 5–10 minutes (not including cooking the quinoa)

2 handfuls baby spinach

¼ cup (35 g) chopped cucumber

2 tbsp (18 g) golden raisins

1 tbsp (8 g) sesame seeds

2 tbsp (18 g) sunflower seeds

2 tbsp (18 g) pumpkin seeds

¼ cup (47 g) cooked quinoa*

½ an avocado, sliced

½ cup (40 g) mandarin orange sections

DRESSING (OR USE CLOSEST
STORE-BOUGHT VARIATION)

2 tbsp (30 ml) extra virgin olive oil

2 tbsp (30 ml) fresh lemon juice

2 tsp (30 g) Dijon mustard

2 tsp (18 g) poppy seeds

¼ tsp onion powder

1 tbsp (15 ml) apple cider vinegar

2 pitted dates, soaked 30 minutes
(healthier) or ½ tsp agave

¼ tsp black pepper

Pinch of sea salt

Toss together the spinach, cucumber, raisins, sesame seeds, sunflower seeds, pumpkin seeds and quinoa. Place the salad on your plate and add the avocado slices and orange sections on top.

Blend (if you are using dates) or whisk (if you are using agave) together the dressing ingredients. Pour the dressing on top of the salad and enjoy!

*For instructions on how to cook quinoa see page 44.

MINDFUL MEDITERRANEAN *Salad*

This Mediterranean-inspired dish is anything but dull. Layered with tangy, sharp and sweet ingredients, it has all the character and sass of the Greek isles. The chickpeas will keep up that healthy digestion, helping you speed up your weight loss and it matches beautifully with the creamy, rich tahini dressing. This type of dressing is commonly found in health food sections of stores, so if you need or want to reduce the creation time, grab a bottle when you shop.

Servings: 1 | **Prep time:** 10–15 minutes | **Creation time:** 5–10 minutes

4–6 cups (220–330 g) chopped romaine hearts

½ cup (70 g) chopped cucumber

½ cup (90 g) chopped tomato

¼ cup (40 g) chopped red onion

¼ cup (25 g) black olive slices

¼ cup (75 g) chopped artichoke hearts

2 tbsp (8 g) finely chopped fresh parsley

¾–1 cup (180–240 g) chickpeas

2 tbsp (18 g) sunflower seeds, optional

TAHINI DRESSING (OR USE CLOSEST STORE-BOUGHT VERSION)

1 tbsp (15 ml) extra virgin olive oil

1 tbsp (15 g) tahini

1 tbsp (15 ml) fresh lemon juice

1 tbsp (15 ml) apple cider vinegar

1 clove garlic, minced

½ tbsp (2 g) flat-leaf parsley, finely chopped

⅛ tsp salt

Splash of water, optional

Place all of the chopped vegetables in a large bowl with the chickpeas.

In a small bowl, whisk together all the dressing ingredients, adding water if you prefer a thinner consistency.

Toss the dressing with the vegetables, sprinkle the optional sunflower seeds on top and serve immediately.

SMOKED EGG-LESS EGG *Salad*

This easy-to-make, protein-packed take on the popular traditional salad overflows with different flavors, tang and spice. It will satisfy your taste buds as well as your tummy. You can enjoy feeling content, light and energized until your next meal. Feel free to make a double portion so that you have easy leftovers you can turn to over the next couple days!

Servings: 1 meal-size portion | **Prep time:** 5–8 minutes (not including pressing the tofu) | **Creation time:** 10 minutes

½ a block of extra-firm tofu, drained and pressed*

EGG-LESS SALAD

1 large celery stalk, chopped

1 green onion stalk, chopped

3–4 tbsp (45–60 g) vegan mayonnaise

⅛ tsp onion powder

2–3 sprigs fresh dill, chopped, or about 1–1½ tsp dried dill

1½ tsp (7 g) capers

⅛ tsp turmeric

⅛ tsp black pepper

Smoked seasoning salt to taste

1 handful chopped romaine lettuce

Splash of extra virgin olive oil

Splash of lemon juice

After draining and pressing the tofu, crumble it using your fingers into a medium-size bowl. Add the rest of the eggless salad ingredients and combine thoroughly.

In a large salad bowl, toss the lettuce with a splash of olive oil and lemon juice.

Add the egg-less salad on top and enjoy.

*See page 43 for instructions on pressing tofu.

TWO BEAN PROTEIN *Chili* WITH SLICED AVOCADO

This is truly the tastiest chili I've ever had and it's super simple to make! The TVP (textured vegetable protein, page 202) makes it just as high in protein as any chili containing meat, but without any of the cholesterol and artery clogging fat! In fact, this chili doesn't even include a drop of oil, making it particularly helpful for you on your journey to a lean, fit body.

Servings: 3–4 meal-size portions | **Prep time:** 10 minutes | **Creation time:** 5 minutes active kitchen time + 8–9 hours of cooking in the slow cooker

3 cups (700 ml) vegetable broth

½ cup (45 g) textured vegetable protein (TVP)

½ a yellow onion, diced

1 (6 oz [165 g]) can tomato paste

1 (14.5 oz [410 g]) can diced tomatoes

½ tsp garlic powder

½ a red bell pepper (or bell pepper of choice)

½ cup (8 g) loosely packed fresh cilantro, chopped

1 tsp chili powder

¼ tsp sea salt to taste

Dash of cayenne to taste

1 (15 oz [425 g]) can kidney beans, drained

1 (15 oz [425 g]) can pinto beans, drained

½ a jalapeño pepper, diced, optional

Avocado slices

Combine all of the ingredients except the beans and avocado in your slow cooker and cook 7 to 8 hours on low.

Add the beans and cook for 1 more hour.

Serve with avocado slices on top or on the side.

WARM ME UP WHITE BEAN *Soup* &
STEAMED ZUCCHINI HALVES

This comforting, creamy soup is easy to make and supports your efforts to strengthen your body from the inside out. The beans add tons of protein and fiber and the celery and rosemary keep things fresh. The spinach provides you with iron and boosts the digestion-aiding properties of this great soup.

A big bowl and you may be happy without a side dish. But if your appetite says, "Give me more," then it will only take you a few minutes and minimal effort to roll out this simple zucchini side.

WARM ME UP WHITE BEAN SOUP

Servings: 3-4 meal-size servings | **Prep time:** 10-15 minutes | **Cook time:** 30 minutes

1 tbsp (15 ml) olive oil

4 cloves garlic, minced

½ a yellow onion, diced

1 green onion, diced, plus more for garnish

2 stalks celery, sliced

½ sprig fresh rosemary leaves, plus more for garnish

2 handfuls spinach, chopped

2 (15 oz [425 g]) cans cannellini beans

¼ tsp Herbamare seasoning

Black pepper to taste

¾ cup (175 ml) unsweetened plain almond, flax or rice milk

Dash of hot sauce, optional

Preheat a large saucepan with the olive oil to medium heat.

Add the garlic, yellow onion, green onion, celery and rosemary, and sauté until tender, about 6 to 8 minutes.

Place the mixture in a high-speed blender.

In the emptied pot, wilt the chopped spinach and then take the pan off the heat.

In the blender with the sauté mixture, add the cannellini beans, Herbamare, black pepper, milk and optional hot sauce, and process until smooth and creamy.

Pour the contents of the blender in the pot with the spinach and stir. Turn the heat to medium and stir occasionally until the soup is heated all the way through.

Serve in a bowl and garnish with diced green onion and fresh rosemary.

STEAMED ZUCCHINI HALVES

Servings: 2 sides | **Prep time:** 2 minutes | **Creation time:** 15 minutes

1 zucchini, destemmed and cut in half lengthwise

½ tbsp (7 ml) extra virgin olive oil or vegan buttery spread

Sea salt to taste

Black pepper to taste

Steam the zucchini halves using a steamer basket in a pot on the stove until fork tender, about 10 to 12 minutes.

Place the zucchini halves on a plate, open-side facing up.

Score the zucchini with a fork and then drizzle with olive oil or buttery spread, and salt and pepper to taste.

BELLA BROCCOLI *Soup* & QUINOA *Side*

This soup is rich and filling and really hits the spot! The cashews create a creamy thickness and also promote healthy gums, teeth, hair and heart, and they can even help with a better night's sleep. The big serving of broccoli will help detox your body, providing a good amount of antioxidants while also protecting your stomach lining. If the broccoli soup is not quite enough to fill your belly for the night, heat up a side of simple quinoa to go along with it.

BELLA BROCCOLI SOUP

Servings: 4 | Prep time: 10 minutes (not including 4–8 hours soaking cashews) | Creation time: 45 minutes stovetop method or 9 hours in the slow cooker + 5 minutes active kitchen time

1 cup (145 g) raw cashews, soaked 4–8 hours if using the stovetop method

4 cups (950 ml) vegetable broth, divided

1 cup (145 g) chopped yellow onion

2–3 cloves garlic, or ½–1 tsp bottled minced garlic

Dash of extra virgin olive oil or olive oil cooking spray

4–5 cups (280–350 g) chopped fresh broccoli

1 cup (235 ml) vegan milk of choice

½ cup (95 g) nutritional yeast

Dash of hot sauce or cayenne pepper to taste, optional

½ tsp sea salt to taste

Black pepper to taste

STOVETOP

Rinse the soaked cashews. Combine them with 2 cups (475 ml) of vegetable broth in a blender and process until smooth.

In a large saucepan, sauté the onions and garlic in the olive oil over low heat. When the onion becomes translucent, about 5 minutes, add the broccoli, stir briefly and add remaining 2 cups (475 ml) of vegetable broth. Bring to a boil, then turn the heat down and simmer until the broccoli becomes soft and begins to change color, about 6 to 8 minutes. Turn the heat off and stir in the milk, the cashews blended with vegetable broth, nutritional yeast, hot sauce or cayenne, salt and pepper. Reheat and serve.

SLOW COOKER

Combine all of the ingredients, except the nutritional yeast and milk, in your slow cooker. Cook on low for about 8 hours.

Add the nutritional yeast and milk and blend thoroughly using an immersion blender, or transfer to a high-speed blender for processing. Continue to cook on low for another 30 minutes to 1 hour.

QUINOA SIDE

Servings: 1 | Prep time: 2 minutes (not including cooking the quinoa) | Creation time: 5 minutes

¾ cup (90 g) quinoa, cooked*

Dash of Herbamare seasoning to taste

Black pepper to taste

½ tbsp (7 ml) of extra virgin olive oil, optional

2–3 sundried tomatoes, diced, optional

¾ cup (90 g) chickpeas or beans of choice, drained and rinsed, optional

Heat the quinoa in a saucepan on the stove or in the microwave with Herbamare seasoning, pepper to taste, and optional olive oil, sundried tomatoes and/or beans.

*For instructions on cooking see page 44.

WASABI CAULIFLOWER *Mash* & EASY BROCCOLI

Never miss mashed potatoes again! Who would have thought you can recreate beloved mashed potatoes with a vegetable as healthy and nutrient-packed as cauliflower? Cauliflower is an exception to the general rule that we should stay away from white foods—it's a nutritional powerhouse! To go alongside this comforting dish are especially easy-to-make protein- and fiber-rich broccoli.

WASABI CAULIFLOWER MASH

Servings: 3 | **Prep time:** 5 minutes | **Creation time:** 25–30 minutes

1 small head of cauliflower

4 cloves garlic, whole

2–3 tbsp Earth Balance buttery spread or sub extra virgin olive oil

½–¾ tsp wasabi powder

¼ tsp sea salt

1 tbsp (4 g) chopped parsley, optional, plus more for garnish

Black pepper to taste

Remove the leaves and hard bottom from the cauliflower.

Cut the remaining cauliflower into pieces so that it will fit in the steamer—the smaller the pieces, the quicker they will cook.

Steam the cauliflower and whole garlic cloves until tender, about 10 minutes.

Preheat the oven to broil.

Combine the cauliflower and garlic with the other ingredients in your high-speed blender and process until smooth. Alternatively, you can place all of the ingredients in a pot or bowl and use an immersion blender to process.

Pour or scoop the mash into a glass pan and broil until it's browned on top, about 5 minutes. Remove and sprinkle with parsley.

EASY BROCCOLI

Servings: 2 side servings | **Prep time:** 2 minutes | **Creation time:** 10 minutes

2 cups (315 g) frozen broccoli florets

3 tbsp (30 g) almond slivers, cashew halves or pine nuts, toasted

½ tbsp (7 ml) extra virgin olive oil or Earth Balance buttery spread

Herbamare seasoning (or regular sea salt) to taste

Black pepper to taste

Steam the broccoli using a steamer basket in a pot on the stove until it's fork tender, about 5 minutes.

Meanwhile, toast the nuts in the toaster oven at 350°F (180°C) for about 3 minutes until slightly browned. This step is optional.

Remove broccoli from the heat and transfer to a bowl.

Add the olive oil or buttery spread and Herbamare or salt and pepper to taste. Sprinkle the nuts on top and enjoy with your Wasabi Cauliflower Mash.

ASIAN *Tofu* WITH SNOW PEAS & BAMBOO SHOOTS

These great flavors make this tofu dish scrumptious. You'll love this digestion aiding meal! Soothing for the stomach and rooted in ancient tradition, bamboo is said to aid in weight loss and fight inflammation and disease. High in protein, low in carbs, hydrating and with sweet notes from the snow peas, you'll be tempted to lick your plate clean!

If you are pressed for time, simply use a premade sauce instead of making it from scratch, just make sure to check the sugar content and avoid chemical additives.

Servings: 1-2 | **Prep time:** 5-10 minutes (not including pressing the tofu) | **Creation time:** 15-20 minutes

½ **block extra-firm tofu, drained and pressed***

1 **tbsp (15 ml) grape seed oil, or sub sesame oil or peanut oil**

1½ **cups (215 g) snow peas, destemmed**

¾ **cup (28 g) canned sliced bamboo shoots, drained and rinsed**

Red pepper flakes to taste, optional

½ **tbsp (4 g) black sesame seeds**

SAUCE (OR USE A SIMILAR STORE-BOUGHT VERSION)

⅔ **cup (155 ml) vegetable broth**

1 **tbsp (15 ml) Braggs Liquid Aminos**

2 **tbsp (30 ml) fresh lemon juice to taste**

⅛ **tsp garlic powder**

⅛ **tsp ginger powder**

1 **tbsp (8 g) cornstarch**

Cut the pressed tofu into small cubes, about ½ inch (1.3 cm).

Add peanut or grape seed oil to a sauté pan or wok and heat to medium-high. Add the tofu and cook, stirring often, for about 5 minutes, until the tofu begins to brown.

Add the snow peas and cook approximately 5 minutes more, or until the snow peas soften.

Add the bamboo shoots and mix everything together.

In a small bowl, whisk together all the sauce ingredients.

In the sauté pan, push the vegetables around the outside, creating space in the center of the pan. Pour the sauce into the center of the pan and stir for about 1 minute until the sauce thickens.

Thoroughly mix together the vegetables and sauce, and add red pepper flakes to taste.

Serve, adding the sesame seeds on top for added crunch.

*See page 43 for instructions on pressing tofu.

FIESTA *Pizza*

Pizza seems to be one of the most craved, least healthy meals there is! Power-up with this healthy, Tex-Mex version of pizza that will not only leave you full and happy, but will ensure you receive a huge amount of essential vitamins and minerals at the same time. Sauté a double portion of the veggies if you're up for it, and enjoy them as part of your luscious leftovers during the week. In fact, throw any veggies that might be on the verge of going bad on this pizza!

Servings: 1 meal-size portion | **Prep time:** 10 minutes | **Creation time:** 15–20 minutes

½ cup (75 g) green pepper slices

½ cup (80 g) red onion slices

1 cup (70 g) mushroom slices

Drop of coconut oil (refined) or grape seed oil

1 large whole grain tortilla, sprouted if available

⅓–½ cup (85–125 g) pizza sauce

½–¾ cup (60–100 g) shredded Daiya mozzarella or pepper jack

½ cup (125 g) canned black beans, drained, rinsed and patted dry

¼ cup (25 g) black olives

½ cup (40 g) vegan beef crumbles* or tempeh bacon, optional

Sauté the green pepper and onion in a large pan with cooking oil spray on medium-high heat. Add the mushrooms when the pepper and onion begin to become tender, about 6 minutes.

When the vegetables are all done cooking, about 8 to 10 minutes total, set the mixture aside.

Heat the drop of oil in a pan on medium heat. Place the tortilla in the pan until the edges become crisp, about 3 minutes, flipping once.

Preheat oven or toaster oven to 375°F (190°C).

Place the whole grain tortilla on parchment paper and spread the pizza sauce evenly on top.

Next, add a layer of the Daiya shreds, the black beans, green peppers, onion, mushrooms, black olives and optional vegan beef crumbles.

Last, sprinkle the rest of the Daiya shreds on top.

Place the pizza on the parchment paper in the oven until the sauce is hot and the Daiya is melted and beginning to bubble, about 5 minutes.

*Recommended brands: Beyond Meat, Gardein, Amy's, Boca

MUSCLE-BUILDING MUNG BEAN *Fettuccini Alfredo*

With stacks of protein—25 grams per serving—and slow-releasing energy, mung bean pasta is a great partner for cauliflower. Together they provide excellent support for the cardiovascular and digestive system as well as creating a hearty and filling meal with tons of fiber. A perfect combo for a clean, plant-powered dinner!

Servings: 2 | **Prep time:** 10 minutes | **Creation time:** 25-30 minutes

CAULIFLOWER ALFREDO SAUCE

3 cups (400 g) cauliflower florets

½ tbsp (7 ml) extra virgin olive oil

3 cloves garlic, minced

2 tbsp (30 ml) vegetable broth

¼ cup (60 ml) vegan milk of choice, plain flavored

1 tbsp (15 g) vegan buttery spread

¼ tsp onion powder

1 tbsp (12 g) nutritional yeast

1 tbsp (15 ml) white wine, or sub ½ tbsp (7 ml) fresh lemon juice

2 tbsp (8 g) chopped fresh parsley, divided

½ tsp sea salt to taste

¼ tsp black pepper to taste

PASTA AND PEAS

1 cup (130 g) frozen green peas

½ a package Explore Asian Edamame & Mung Bean Fettuccini, about 2½ oz (70 g) dry

CAULIFLOWER ALFREDO SAUCE

Add the cauliflower florets to a medium-size pot filled with 1-2 inches (2.5-5 cm) of boiling water.

Reduce the heat, cover and cook for about 12 to 15 minutes or until tender.

Drain the cauliflower using a colander and set aside. You have the option to save a couple tablespoons (30 ml) of the broth to use instead of vegetable broth.

Place the pot back on the stove on medium heat and sauté garlic in olive oil until it starts to brown, 1 to 2 minutes.

Add the vegetable or cauliflower broth, milk, buttery spread, onion powder, nutritional yeast, white wine, 1 tablespoon (4 g) of the parsley, salt and pepper to the cauliflower pot.

Process with an immersion blender until smooth. Add more milk if the sauce is too thick.

Place the burner on low heat, stirring occasionally as you make the peas and pasta.

PASTA & PEAS

Bring a large pot of water to a boil. Add the frozen peas and fettuccini.

Return the water to a boil, reduce heat and cook until al dente, about 5 minutes—the pasta and peas have the same cook time.

Drain using the colander and return to the pot.

Add the sauce, and stir over medium heat until hot.

Sprinkle the rest of the chopped parsley on top once served.

DECADENT CHOCOLATE-RASPBERRY Mousse

This is seriously one of the most rich and delicious desserts I've ever made and it's 100% guilt free! The creamy texture given by the avocado is wonderful. This dessert is bursting with antioxidants and good fats, great for digestion and contains dates as the sweetener, which have even been shown to reduce allergy symptoms, so sneezers eat up!

Servings: 1 large or 2 small portions | **Prep time:** 5 minutes (not including soaking dates) | **Creation time:** 5–10 minutes

2 tbsp (30 g) raw cacao powder, or sub pure cocoa powder

5 pitted dates, soaked 30 minutes (recommended)

1 tsp vanilla

2–4 tbsp (30–60 ml) almond milk (or vegan milk of choice)

1 ripe avocado

½ cup (125 g) frozen raspberries

Pinch of salt

Place all of the ingredients in a high-speed blender and process until totally smooth and creamy. This treat is perfect to enjoy immediately, but it can be stored in the fridge to eat later as well.

PINING FOR PINEAPPLE FROZEN Dessert

There's nothing better than the sweet, unique taste of pineapple. Pineapple has been linked to alleviating joint and arthritis pain, as well as being an important source of many key vitamins and minerals. Mangoes also have similar health benefits. Together, with the muscle-building properties of yogurt, this deliciously fresh-tasting dessert is on your side when it comes to helping you achieve the shape you want.

Servings: 2 | **Prep time:** 5 minutes | **Creation time:** 5–8 minutes

---

½–¾ cup (115–175 g) vegan yogurt

¾ cup (130 g) frozen pineapple chunks

½ cup (90 g) frozen mango

½ a frozen banana

½ a lemon, juiced

Splash of vegan milk, if needed

Combine all of the ingredients in a high-speed blender and process until fully blended. Add milk only if the mixture won't blend and needs some liquid. Eat right away for the best texture.

WEEK 3

OVERVIEW

	MON	TUES	WED	THURS	FRI	SAT	SUN
BREAKFAST	Wonderful Watermelon Smoothie	Cinnamon Bun Smoothie	Lively Lemon Basil Smoothie	Ramp Up Raspberry Cacao Smoothie	So Fresh & So Clean Smoothie	Let's Toast!	Gorgeous Grits
LUNCH	Kiss Me Kale & Apple Salad	Luscious Leftovers	Save-The-Chicken Salad	Luscious Leftovers	Salad with a Kick	Luscious Leftovers	
SNACK	Fresh Fruit of Choice	Fresh Fruit of Choice	Fresh Fruit of Choice	Fresh Fruit of Choice	Fresh Fruit of Choice	Fresh Fruit of Choice	Fresh Fruit of Choice
DINNER	Zesty Zucchini Basil Soup with Quinoa Side	Maple Baked Carrots & Lemon Garlic Asparagus	Flirty Farro Soup & Baby Bok Choy	Tex-Mex Cauliflower Couscous & Thyme Green Beans	Kickass Carrot Ginger Soup & Cucumber Dill Salad	Epic Eggplant Mushroom Casserole with White Bean Sauce	Big Pimpin' Portobello Burger & Edamame
TREAT	X	X	Sweetie Pie Pudding	X	X	X	Playful PB Chocolate Chip Frozen Dessert
WORKOUT	Cross-Train (full body focus)	Cardio + Yoga	Cross-Train (upper body focus)	Cardio	Cross-Train (lower body focus)	Yoga + Cardio	Off/Rest

GROCERY LIST - WEEK 3

LIQUIDS

- Coconut milk, culinary (¾ cup [175 ml]) or full fat (1¼ cups
- [295 ml])
- Coconut water (1 cup [235 ml])
- Vegan milk of choice (48 oz [1.4 L])
- Vegetable broth (96 oz [2.85 L])

FRUIT

- Apple (1)
- Avocado (1)
- Bananas (6)
- Lemons (4)
- Lime (1) or sub lime juice
- Pears (2)
- Strawberries (6–8)
- Watermelon cubes (2½ cups [375 g])
- Frozen raspberries (1 cup [280 g])
- Dates (9)
- Goji berries (1 tbsp [9 g])
- Golden raisins (2 tbsp [18 g])

LEAFY GREENS

- Baby spinach (2 handfuls)
- Kale, lacinato (not curly) (1 bunch)
- Romaine lettuce (3 hearts)
- Boston lettuce or salad greens of choice (1 handful)

VEGETABLES

- Asparagus (1 bunch)
- Baby bok choy (2 stalks)
- Bell peppers of choice (1)
- Bean sprouts (¼ cup [15 g])
- Carrot (2 lb [900 g])
- Celery (1 stalk)
- Cauliflower (1½ heads)
- Cucumber (1½)
- Dandelion greens (or spinach) (1 handful)
- Eggplant (1)
- Green beans (4 cups [485 g])
- Mushrooms (1–1½ packages [8 oz (225–335 g)] each)
- Mushrooms, portobello caps (2)
- Onion, green (2 stalks)
- Onion, yellow (3)
- Red/purple cabbage, shredded (½ cup [45 g])
- Sundried tomatoes (2)
- Sweet potato or yam (1½)
- Tomato (1)
- Wakame, dried (seaweed) (¼ cup [28 g])
- Zucchini (2 large)
- Diced tomatoes (one 14.5-oz [410-g] can)
- Red pasta sauce (1 cup [245 g])
- Roasted red pepper slices (a few)
- Dill pickle sandwich slices (a few), optional
- Fresh basil (½ oz [15 g])
- Fresh cilantro (¼ cup [4 g])
- Fresh dill (¼ oz [7 g])
- Fresh mint (½ oz [15 g])
- Fresh parsley (½ cup [30 g])
- Fresh thyme (¼ oz [7 g]) or sub dried
- Garlic cloves (1 bulb)
- Ginger, fresh (1 tbsp [8 g]), diced

NUTS/SEEDS

- Almond slivers (3 tbsp [30 g])
- Pecan pieces (⅓ cup [50 g])
- Walnut halves (¼ cup [40 g])

LEGUMES

- Edamame, frozen shelled (½ cup [60 g])
- Edamame, frozen in pod (2 cups [235 g])
- Beyond Meat brand Beyond Chicken Grilled Strips (8) or tempeh (½ package)
- Vegan sausage crumbles, tempeh bacon, or Bac'Un bits—optional
- Black beans (½ a 15-oz [425-g] can)
- Great Northern beans (one 15-oz [425 g] can)

VEGAN DAIRY

- Daiya shreds, optional

WHOLE GRAIN

- Yellow grits, whole grain (¼ cup [40 g])
- Whole grain toast, sprouted if available (2)
- Sprouted whole grain bun, sprouted if available

PREP DAY

- Cook quinoa
- Chop vegetables for salads and soups

WONDERFUL WATERMELON *Smoothie*

Sweet with a burst of minty fresh flavor, this refreshing smoothie will wake up your digestive system, making a perfect kick-off to your day. Mint leaves promote healthy digestion by relaxing the muscles that line your digestive tract. Watermelon is also a nutrient-dense, hydrating food that has been shown to aid in recovery following exercise, as well as reducing muscle soreness.

Servings: 1 | **Prep time:** 5 minutes (if you buy precut watermelon, 10 minutes if you cut your own) | **Creation time:** 2 minutes

2½–3 cups (375–450 g) watermelon cubes	Combine all of the ingredients in a high-speed blender and process until smooth.
1 ripe pear, cored	
½ a frozen banana	
2 tbsp (16 g) hemp seeds	
5 mint leaves to taste	
1 tsp amla powder, optional	
1 tbsp (15 g) maca powder, optional	

LIVELY LEMON BASIL *Smoothie*

This green smoothie has a great citrus kick and refreshing basil taste. A perfect detoxing start to your morning that will set you up with energy to take on the day! Dandelion greens give a spike in calcium and iron, as well as promoting insulin production in the body, keeping blood sugar low. The greens also have a diuretic effect to help rid your body of extra water weight. This smoothie is stuffed full of essential vitamins and minerals for all-around good health. I recommend adding amla powder to exponentially increase the antioxidant level as well.

Servings: 1 | **Prep time:** 8-10 minutes | **Creation time:** 2 minutes

1 large lemon or 2 smaller lemons, peeled and deseeded

1 pear, cored, or sub apple, cored

½ a cucumber

½ a frozen banana

1 small handful dandelion greens, or sub handful spinach

4-5 large basil leaves

1 cup (235 ml) coconut water

2 tbsp (16 g) hemp seeds

1 tsp amla powder, optional

1 tbsp (15 g) maca powder, optional

Combine all of the ingredients in a high-speed blender and process until smooth.

CINNAMON BUN Smoothie

Did somebody say cinnamon bun? Yum! Smooth, sweet, nutty and filling, this smoothie will top off your potassium levels and provide slow-releasing energy to keep hunger at bay for longer. Cinnamon is also surprisingly beneficial. It helps regulate blood sugar and improves heart health and cognitive function.

Servings: 1 | **Prep time:** 2 minutes | **Creation time:** 2 minutes

1½ cups (355 ml) almond milk	Combine all of the ingredients in a high-speed blender and process until smooth.
1 tsp cinnamon to taste	
1 tsp vanilla extract	
1 large frozen banana	
1 tbsp (15 g) almond butter	
1 tbsp (7 g) pecan pieces	
5 pitted dates	
¼ cup (20 g) oats	
Stevia to taste, optional	
1 tsp amla powder, optional	

SO FRESH & SO CLEAN Smoothie

Great greenery! This muscle-building smoothie will wake up your taste buds and is great for enhancing a workout—it gives your body a big dose of protein from the vegan protein powder. Thanks to the mint, this smoothie can reduce cravings for sweet treats while aiding digestion and soothing an inflamed stomach.

Servings: 1 | **Prep time:** 2 minutes | **Creation time:** 2 minutes

2 cups (475 ml) vegan milk of choice	Blend all of the ingredients in a high-speed blender until smooth. Adjust the milk amount to reach the thickness you desire.
1 handful spinach	
¼ cup (24 g) loosely packed mint leaves to taste	
½ tbsp (7 g) raw cacao	
1 scoop raw vegan protein powder, plain flavored	
Stevia to taste	
2 ice cubes	

RAMP UP RASPBERRY CACAO *Smoothie*

This delicious addition to the menu will fill you with fiber, provide a great boost to your metabolism and give you plenty of energy. It's a bit like drinking your dessert. If you have a weakness for chocolate, you can give in to your weakness without compromising the progress you've made toward flat abs.

Servings: 1 | **Prep time:** 5 minutes | **Creation time:** 2 minutes

1–2 tbsp (15–30 g) raw cacao or unsweetened Dutch-processed cocoa powder

1 cup (250 g) frozen raspberries

3 tbsp (24 g) hemp seeds

½–1 banana, frozen or fresh

2 pitted dates

1½–2 cups (355–475 ml) vegan milk of choice

Stevia to taste, optional

½–1 scoop vegan protein powder, optional

Combine all of the ingredients in a high-speed blender and process until smooth.

GORGEOUS GRITS

For a highly substantial and satisfying start to your Sunday, try this recipe! It's a delicious combination of ground corn and sautéed vegetables, made creamy with vegan cheese, and has the option to boost protein levels and flavor with vegan sausage or bacon. This brunch is somewhat of a special treat because of its inclusion of vegan cheese and faux meat, but not so much that you shouldn't have it—you deserve a bit of a reward for a week of incredibly healthy eating! And this reward still provides you with a good mix of essential vitamins and minerals while getting your stomach to work, keeping your metabolic system speedy.

If you are missing one or more of the vegetables, don't let it deter you from creating the dish with what you have. These grits will taste great with a number of combinations of different sautéed vegetables, so give it a shot!

Servings: 1 brunch-size portion | **Prep time:** 10 minutes | **Creation time:** 15–30 minutes

1 cup (235 ml) vegetable broth (salt-free) or sub water

¼ tsp sea salt to taste

¼ cup (40 g) whole grain yellow speckled/stone ground grits

Touch of extra virgin olive oil

½ cup (80 g) chopped yellow onion

½ cup (75 g) sliced bell peppers of choice

2 sundried tomatoes, diced

¾ cup (50 g) sliced mushrooms

½ tbsp (7 ml) extra virgin olive oil (healthier) or Earth Balance buttery spread

¼ cup (20 g) Daiya shreds or sub 1–2 tbsp (5–10 g) nutritional yeast

Black pepper to taste

OPTIONAL ADDITIONS

Hot sauce to taste

⅓ cup (35 g) cooked vegan sausage crumbles

2 chopped vegan tempeh bacon strips

Vegan Bac'Un bits* to taste

Bring the vegetable broth and sea salt to a boil in a medium saucepan.

Add the grits, bring the broth back to a boil, reduce the heat to medium-low/low and cook according to the directions—depending on the exact type of grits, this could range from 7 to 25 minutes.

Meanwhile, in a skillet, sauté the vegetables in olive oil over medium heat. Start by sautéing the onion for 3 to 5 minutes, then add the bell pepper and tomato, sautéing for another 3 to 5 minutes, and last adding the mushrooms until all are tender, another 3 to 5 minutes.

Add the sautéed vegetables, Earth Balance, Daiya shreds, black pepper, and optional hot sauce, vegan sausage crumbles, tempeh bacon and/or Bac'Un bits to the grits and serve.

*Recommended products: Lightlife Gimme Lean Ground Sausage, Lightlife Fakin' Bacon, Frontier Bac'Uns

LET'S Toast!

Here's a toast to looking and feeling your best! Fill yourself up with this delectable combination of grains, nuts and fruit. This meal will start your day with timed-release energy hiding in the guise of a tasty treat—yum, yum!

Servings: 1-2 | **Prep time:** 5-8 minutes | **Creation time:** 10 minutes

2 slices whole grain toast, preferably sprouted grain

3 tbsp (50 g) almond butter

½–1 banana, sliced, optional

¾ cup (128 g) fresh strawberries, sliced

1 tbsp (15 g) goji berries

1 tbsp (15 g) unsweetened coconut shreds

First, toast the bread and then spread the almond butter on the slices.

Add the banana slices if you choose to include banana, followed by the strawberry slices.

Sprinkle the goji berries and coconut shreds on top and enjoy!

KISS ME KALE & APPLE *Salad*

Sink your teeth into this tangy and sweet vitamin C-filled salad! It's easy to make, keeps well for a few days in the fridge—so I recommend you make extra for leftovers—and is surprisingly fulfilling.

Servings: 1 | **Prep time:** 10 minutes | **Creation time:** 5 minutes

DRESSING

½ a lemon, juiced

1 tbsp (15 ml) extra virgin olive oil

1 tbsp (15 ml) apple cider vinegar

⅛–¼ tsp sea salt

Black pepper to taste

4 cups (270 g) chopped lacinato kale (not curly)

1 carrot, shredded

½ an apple, chopped into small bite size pieces

2 tbsp (18 g) golden raisins

1 tbsp (4 g) chopped fresh dill, chopped

¼ cup (30 g) walnut halves

In a small bowl, make the dressing by whisking together the lemon juice, olive oil, vinegar and salt. Add the black pepper to taste.

Place the chopped kale in a large bowl and add the dressing mixture. Using your hands, massage the dressing into the kale for several minutes.

Next, add the carrots, apple, raisins and dill, and mix them thoroughly.

Allow the salad to sit for at least 15 minutes, preferably longer, to give the kale time to soften.

Mix the walnuts into the salad just before eating so that they stay nice and crunchy.

SAVE-THE-CHICKEN *Salad*

This high-protein recipe is a spin-off of traditional chicken salad. The real surprise in this dish isn't just that it's free of meat, it's actually the addition of capers, which give the salad an extra zing of flavor! If the product Beyond Meat Chicken-less Strips by Hampton Creek is available in your neighborhood, you will barely be able to tell the difference because it mocks chicken so closely. If not, don't worry! This dish is delicious when made with tempeh as well. You can enjoy this salad alone, over greens as it appears in the meal plan, in a sandwich or in lettuce wraps to reduce carbs.

Servings: 1 complete lunch salad + 1–2 leftover servings of the Save-the-Chicken Salad | **Prep time:** 10 minutes | **Creation time:** 10–15 minutes

8 strips of Beyond Meat Grilled Chicken-less strips (Hampton Creek brand)

OR

½ (4 oz [115 g]) package tempeh and olive oil cooking spray

2 tbsp (30 g) vegan mayonnaise*

¼ of a lemon, juiced

1 tbsp (9 g) capers

1 celery stalk

¼ cup (40 g) green onion, chopped

½ (75 g) cup red bell pepper, chopped

2 cups (110 g) chopped romaine lettuce

Splash of extra virgin olive oil

Sea salt and pepper

If you are using the Beyond Meat, slice the chicken-less strips into ½-inch (1.3-cm) pieces and put to the side.

If you are using tempeh, slice it into ½–¾-inch (1.3–2-cm) cubes. Heat a skillet with olive oil spray and fry the tempeh according to the directions on the package. Remove from the heat and place in the refrigerator to cool.

Meanwhile, in a medium-size container with a top, mix together the mayonnaise, lemon juice and capers. Add the celery, green onion, red pepper and chicken-less strips or tempeh. Put the top on the container and shake until thoroughly combined.

Toss the chopped lettuce in a bowl with a splash of olive oil and a dash of salt and pepper.

Place the lettuce on a large plate and top with a portion of the Save-The-Chicken Salad.

Store the leftovers in a sealed container in the fridge.

*Recommended brands include Hampton Creek's Just Mayo and Follow Your Heart Vegenaise

Salad WITH A KICK

For a playful assault on your taste buds, try this colorful and nutrient-filled salad. Bursting with crunch and hitting the mark for a kick from the wasabi, this salad holds a great freshness to round it all off. Wakame is a type of seaweed and a great source of magnesium, iodine, absorbable calcium, iron and a range of vitamins—so dig in!

Servings: 1 lunch-size portion | **Prep time:** 10-15 minutes | **Creation time:** 10-15 minutes

½ cup (78 g) edamame, shelled

1 handful chopped romaine

1 handful Boston lettuce or greens of choice

½ cup (60 g) sliced cucumber

½ cup (90 g) chopped tomato

½ cup (35 g) shredded purple cabbage

½ cup (75 g) sliced orange, yellow, and/or red bell pepper

¼ cup (12 g) bean sprouts

1 tbsp (8 g) black sesame seeds

¼ cup (28 g) dried wakame

DRESSING

1 tbsp (15 ml) sesame oil

2 tbsp (30 ml) Braggs Liquid Aminos

1 tbsp (15 g) tahini

1 tbsp (15 g) wasabi paste to taste

1 tbsp (15 ml) apple cider vinegar

Bring a pot of water to boil. Add the edamame, reduce heat and cook at a rolling boil—around 6 to 8 minutes—then drain and cool in the fridge.

In a small bowl, whisk together the dressing ingredients.

In a large bowl, combine the lettuce, cucumber, tomato, cabbage, bell pepper, sprouts and edamame.

Toss the dressing with the salad, then add the black sesame seeds and wakame on top.

ZESTY ZUCCHINI BASIL *Soup* WITH QUINOA *Side*

This soup is especially easy and quick to make and surprisingly low in oil considering its creamy thickness. The freshness of the basil, combined with the immune-boosting garlic, really hits the spot. Including a simple side of quinoa rounds off the meal and will have you going to bed satisfied.

ZESTY ZUCCHINI BASIL SOUP

Servings: 2 meal-size portions | **Prep time:** 10 minutes | **Creation time:** 15–20 minutes

2 large zucchini, cut in 2" (5-cm) pieces

1 cup (130 g) cauliflower florets

2 garlic cloves, minced

½ tbsp (7 ml) grape seed oil

1 yellow or white onion, chopped

4–5 large fresh basil leaves

¼–½ tsp sea salt to taste

Black pepper to taste

½–1 cup (120–235 ml) vegetable broth or water

Steam the zucchini and cauliflower until tender, about 7 to 10 minutes.

In a sauté pan, sauté the garlic with the grape seed oil on medium-high heat for a minute and then add the chopped onion. Sauté until the onion becomes translucent and tender, about 5 minutes.

Combine the sautéed onion and garlic with all of the other ingredients in a high-speed blender and process until smooth. Start with ½ cup (120 ml) vegetable broth and add more if necessary to achieve the desired thickness.

QUINOA SIDE

Servings: 1 | **Prep time:** 2 minutes (20 minutes if you have to cook the quinoa) | **Creation time:** 5 minutes

¾ cup (140 g) quinoa, cooked

Dash of Herbamare seasoning to taste

OPTIONAL ADDITIONS

Touch of extra virgin olive oil

Black pepper to taste

1 tbsp (9 g) sunflower seeds

Fresh parsley to taste

Heat the quinoa in a saucepan on the stove or in the microwave with the Herbamare, optional olive oil and pepper to taste. Add in the optional sunflower seeds and parsley before serving.

*For quinoa cooking instructions see page 44.

MAPLE BAKED CARROTS & LEMON GARLIC *Asparagus*

It's fun to mix it up and add some sweetness to your dinners every now and then. Enjoy the rich flavor of roasted carrots enhanced by sweet maple, nutty pecans and delicious cinnamon. Carrots are full of beta-carotene and high in antioxidants.

The full flavor of asparagus is at its peak when complemented with aromatic garlic and zingy lemon.

MAPLE BAKED CARROTS

Servings: 2 large portions | **Prep time:** 5-10 minutes | **Creation time:** 35–45 minutes

1 tbsp (14 g) coconut oil, melted

1 tbsp (15 ml) maple syrup

¼ tsp cinnamon (or to taste)

Sea salt to taste

6 large carrots, sliced into bite-size pieces

¼ cup (30 g) pecan pieces

Preheat oven to 350°F (180°C).

In a large bowl, whisk together the coconut oil, maple syrup, cinnamon and salt. Add the carrots and toss so that the carrots are evenly coated.

Place the coated carrots in a glass baking pan and cook 30 to 40 minutes until the carrots are tender, adding the pecan pieces after about 20 minutes.

LEMON GARLIC ASPARAGUS

Servings: 2 | **Prep time:** 5 minutes | **Creation time:** 10 minutes

½ tbsp (7 ml) extra virgin olive oil

1 garlic clove, minced

1 bunch of asparagus (about 14 oz [410 g]), trimmed

¼ of a large lemon, juiced

Sea salt to taste

Black pepper to taste

Heat a skillet with the olive oil to medium heat. Add the minced garlic and sauté for about a minute.

Place the trimmed asparagus in the pan. Cook, stirring occasionally, until the asparagus is crisp, tender and lightly browned, about 8 to 10 minutes.

Add the lemon juice, salt and pepper and sauté for another 30 seconds before serving.

FLIRTY FARRO *Soup* & BABY BOK CHOY

This soup not only offers many important vitamins and minerals, but it will also keep you full while helping you lose weight through improved digestive and metabolic systems. The high fiber content of the farro, kale and cannellini beans promotes healthy digestion, and the kale is also especially effective at aiding in detoxing and fat burning. This soup is as delicious as it is filling, and the slow cooker will also bring out the rich flavors this recipe has to offer.

It you've never experienced baby bok choy, you're in for a treat with this side dish.

FLIRTY FARRO SOUP

Servings: 4 dinner-size servings | **Prep time:** 5–10 minutes | **Creation time:** 8–10 hours in slow cooker + 5 minutes active kitchen time

1 cup (170 g) farro, rinsed	Place all the ingredients except the cannellini beans in the slow cooker. Cook on the low setting for 8 to 10 hours.
8 cups (1.8 L) vegetable broth	Add the beans to the soup and cook another 30 minutes.
2 cups (135 g) chopped kale	
1 (14.05 oz [410 g]) can diced tomatoes	
1 tbsp (8 g) Italian seasoning	
½ cup (30 g) fresh parsley leaves	
½ a yellow onion, chopped	
½ a large lemon, juiced	
½ tsp sea salt	
Black pepper to taste	
1 (15 oz [425 g]) can cannellini beans, drained and rinsed	

BABY BOK CHOY

Servings: 2 sides | **Prep time:** 5 minutes | **Creation time:** 10 minutes

Ingredients	Instructions
SAUCE (OR USE SIMILAR STORE-BOUGHT VERSION)	In a small bowl, whisk together the sauce ingredients.
2 tbsp (30 ml) Liquid Bragg Aminos or sub tamari	Preheat a small sauté pan with sesame oil to medium-high.
1½ tbsp (24 ml) lemon juice	Chop the baby bok choy by cutting it several times lengthwise and then across into small pieces.
½ tsp garlic powder	Add the bok choy to the pan, starting with the stalks, and then after a minute or two, add the leaves. Sauté until the stalks begin to become tender, about 5 to 8 total minutes.
½ tsp cornstarch	
1 tsp sesame oil	Add the sauce and sauté another 2 minutes or until fork tender.
2 stalks baby bok choy, chopped	Add the sesame seeds and serve warm.
1 tsp black sesame seeds, optional	

KICKASS CARROT GINGER *Soup*
& CUCUMBER DILL *Salad*

With great color and an enticing aroma, this soup aids digestion and promotes weight loss. The addition of chili, ginger and garlic also make it an immune-system-boosting power soup to keep your health in tip-top shape, as well as your figure!

You have two options for creating this soup: stovetop or slow cooker. The stovetop version requires more time and effect in the kitchen, but it turns out great and you can make it the same night you want to eat it. The slow cooker version cuts your effort and work time in the kitchen by a bunch, but you must plan ahead! The choice is yours.

The dill in the fresh cucumber salad makes all the difference in turning something so simple into something so delightful.

KICKASS CARROT GINGER SOUP

1 tsp coconut oil (refined) or coconut oil cooking spray

2 garlic cloves, diced

½ a yellow onion, chopped

1 green onion, chopped, optional

1 lb (455 g) carrots, sliced

½–1 tbsp (3–6 g) diced fresh ginger

2 cups (475 ml) vegetable broth

1–1½ tsp ground cumin

¼ tsp chili powder

1 cup (235 ml) coconut milk

½ tsp sea salt

Black pepper to taste

STOVETOP

Servings: 4 dinner-size servings | **Prep time:** 10 minutes | **Creation time:** 30 minutes

Heat a saucepan with the coconut oil to medium-high.

Add the garlic, then the onion and last, the carrots and ginger. Sauté for about 4 minutes.

Add vegetable broth, cumin and chili powder, and bring to a boil. Reduce the heat, cover and simmer until carrots are tender, about 12 minutes.

Add the coconut milk, salt and pepper and process with an immersion blender until smooth. Add more chili powder, salt and/or pepper to taste.

SLOW COOKER

Servings: 4 dinner-size servings | **Prep time:** 10 minutes | **Creation time:** Up to 6 hours cooking in the slow cooker + 5 minutes active kitchen time

Place all of the ingredients, except the coconut oil, in the slow cooker. Cook on low for 5 to 6 hours, or high for 2½ to 3 hours.

Process with an immersion blender until smooth.

Add more chili powder, salt and/or pepper to taste.

CUCUMBER DILL SALAD

Servings: 2 | **Prep time:** 5 minutes | **Creation time:** 2 minutes

1 large cucumber, sliced lengthwise and finely sliced crosswise

1-2 tbsp (4-8 g) chopped fresh dill or to taste

½-1 tbsp (7-15 ml) extra virgin olive oil

1 tbsp (15 ml) white wine vinegar, or sub apple cider vinegar

Sea salt and pepper to taste

Toss all of the ingredients together and serve.

EPIC EGGPLANT MUSHROOM Casserole WITH WHITE BEAN SAUCE

This is a great "one-dish dinner" that's easy to make and rewarding to eat. Eggplant is mineral rich, providing some nutrients not widely found in other vegetables, as well as being original in texture and taste. The mushrooms and bean sauce add layers of different enjoyable textures. The red sauce addition creates a lasagna-like feel, but it is free of bad carbs and doesn't have any oil!

Servings: 3 large portions | **Prep time:** 10 minutes | **Creation time:** 35–45 minutes (half of which is oven time)

1 large eggplant

1½ cups (375 g) organic red pasta sauce

2½ cups (165 g) sliced white mushrooms

WHITE BEAN SAUCE

1 (15 oz [425 g]) can Great Northern Beans

1 tsp Italian seasoning

⅛ tsp garlic powder

1½ tbsp (18 g) nutritional yeast

1 cup (30 g) spinach, firmly packed

1 tsp dried chives

¼ tsp salt

⅛ tsp cayenne pepper, optional

Preheat the oven to 400°F (200°C).

Peel the eggplant and slice it into ¼-inch (6.5-mm) slices. Place the slices in a single layer on a baking sheet lined with parchment paper and sprinkle the slices with salt. Place the eggplant in the oven and bake until the slices are partially dehydrated and slightly browned. When done, remove from the oven and then turn the oven to 425°F (220°C).

Meanwhile, make the bean sauce by putting the sauce ingredients in a blender or food processor and process until fully blended.

Grease a casserole dish with oil and pour a thin, even layer of red pasta sauce into the dish.

Place half the eggplant slices in a single layer on the sauce.

Next, spread the bean sauce over the eggplant slices.

Place the mushroom slices on top of the bean sauce.

Add another thin layer of red sauce, followed by the rest of the eggplant slices, bean sauce and mushrooms and top with a final layer of red sauce.

Bake uncovered at 425°F (220°C) until fully cooked, about 20 to 25 minutes.

TEX-MEX CAULIFLOWER *Couscous* & THYME GREEN BEANS

It may surprise you that it's possible to get the feeling of eating rice using a vegetable, but this dish proves it true! The cauliflower is packed with nutrients, the beans add plenty of protein, the garlic will help boost your immune system and the cilantro will aid your digestion.

This is a calorie-light dish that will fill you up and invite your tongue to explore novel textures. If you add the optional avocado slices to the dish, it may be enough of a meal that you will want to save the side of green beans for another day. The green beans accented with thyme and almonds, however, do make a perfect clean and green addition to the meal. The recipe calls for either fresh green beans or frozen to make for a quicker creation time, so choose whichever you prefer!

TEX-MEX CAULIFLOWER COUSCOUS

Servings: 2 large portions | **Prep time:** 10–15 minutes | **Creation time:** 12–15 minutes

1 small head of cauliflower

1 tbsp (15 ml) extra virgin olive oil

3 cloves garlic, minced

1 small onion, diced

½ a 15-oz (425-g) can of black beans, drained and rinsed

¼ cup (4 g) chopped cilantro leaves

½ tbsp (7 ml) fresh lime juice, or to taste

1 green onion, minced

¼ tsp sea salt to taste

Black pepper to taste

Dash of cayenne pepper, optional

A few spoonfuls of salsa

½ an avocado, sliced, optional

Cut the leaves and stem from the cauliflower head and discard.

Chop the cauliflower into smaller florets and place them in the food processor. Process until the cauliflower becomes couscous-size pieces: ¼–½ the size of rice.

Heat a skillet with the olive oil to medium heat and sauté the garlic and onion until the onion becomes translucent and slightly tender, about 5 minutes.

Add the cauliflower, black beans, cilantro, lime juice, green onion, salt, pepper and optional dash of cayenne. Stir to coat with oil. Cook for 8 to 10 minutes, stirring occasionally.

Serve with salsa and avocado slices.

(continued)

THYME GREEN BEANS

Servings: 2-3 side portions | **Prep time:** 10-12 minutes using fresh, 5-8 for frozen green beans | **Creation time:** 15 minutes

4 cups (400 g) fresh green beans, destemmed, or frozen green beans

2-3 tbsp (18-27 g) almond slivers

1 tbsp (15 ml) extra virgin olive oil (healthier) or vegan buttery spread

1 clove garlic, minced

2 tbsp (5 g) chopped fresh thyme, or 1 tsp dried thyme

Sea salt and pepper to taste

If you're using fresh green beans, bring a large pot of water to a boil, add the green beans and cook at a rolling boil for 5 to 7 minutes, until crisp-tender.

If you are using frozen beans, steam according to the directions on the package.

Meanwhile, toast the almond slivers in a single layer in a toaster oven set to 350°F (180°C) until slightly browned, about 3 minutes.

Add the olive oil or buttery spread and garlic to a sauté pan and heat to medium-high. Once the garlic begins to brown, add the cooked beans, thyme, salt and pepper. Sauté this for a minute or two.

Place in a serving bowl and sprinkle with the almond slivers.

BIG PIMPIN' PORTOBELLO *Burger* & EDAMAME

This portobello burger is a nutritious and low-calorie alternative to the unhealthy American classic. The "meaty" texture of the portobello mushroom has a lot to do with its ability to act as a burger replacement. If you have a grill or griddle, this is definitely the way to go when it comes to cooking the portobello, but using a pan on the stove works as well. By adding a big helping of edamame to the meal, you will have all your essential amino acids covered! The meal plan calls for you to use only half a whole grain bun for the bottom and use lettuce as the top. This cuts the carbs and calories a great deal and will contribute to quicker loss of body fat.

BIG PIMPIN' PORTOBELLO BURGER

Servings: 2 | **Prep time:** 10 minutes + 30 minutes to marinate mushrooms | **Creation time:** 15 minutes

2 portobello mushroom caps

MARINADE

1 tbsp (15 ml) olive oil

1 tbsp (15 g) tamari or Bragg Liquid Aminos

2 tbsp (30 ml) balsamic vinegar

SAUCE

1 tbsp (15 g) vegan mayonnaise

1 tbsp (15 g) ketchup

½ tbsp (15 g) Dijon mustard

A few dashes of hot sauce to taste

A few roasted red pepper pieces, jarred

1 sprouted whole grain bun, or sub sprouted whole grain bread

½ a large tomato of choice, sliced

½ an avocado, sliced

Dill pickle sandwich slices to taste

2 large romaine lettuce leaves

1 tsp spicy brown mustard

Wipe the mushrooms clean with a damp paper towel; remove the stems and place in a plastic baggie.

In a small bowl, whisk together the marinade ingredients.

Pour the marinade into the baggie with the mushroom caps. Seal the baggie and distribute the liquid around the mushrooms, lay flat and allow to sit for 30 minutes to 2 hours.

In a small bowl, thoroughly combine the mayo, ketchup, mustard and hot sauce and set aside.

If you have a grill or an electric griddle, grill the mushrooms on medium-high heat. Grill the roasted red pepper slices alongside the mushrooms for about 5 minutes on each side or until slightly charred.

Or, in a heavy frying pan set to medium heat—no need for oil since there is some in the marinade—cook 5 minutes on the round side and 2 or 3 on the hollow side, heating the roasted red pepper alongside the caps.

Once you've flipped the mushrooms and they are cooking on the second side, toast the bun, separated into halves.

Spread the sauce onto the bun. Add one portobello cap, followed by red pepper slices, tomato, avocado and pickles.

Place the folded romaine leaves on top, which will create the top half of the bun.

(continued)

EDAMAME

Servings: 2 side portions | **Prep time:** 2 minutes | **Creation time:** 8 minutes

2 cups (300 g) frozen edamame in the pod

Sea salt to taste

Bring a large pot of water to boil.

Add the frozen edamame and boil 5 to 7 minutes until the beans inside the pods are tender—you will want to take one out to try it.

Drain the peas and place in a serving bowl. Sprinkle with sea salt to taste.

To eat, put the pod in your mouth holding one end of the pod. Gently bite down just enough to be able to drag your teeth, pulling the beans out of the pod and into your mouth.

SWEETIE PIE Pudding

This is like pumpkin pie in a bowl! It's sweetened with banana, dates and a bit of maple syrup, and made creamy and rich with coconut milk. All the satisfaction of pudding without any of the unhealthy ingredients that keep us from reaching our health and fitness goals.

Servings: 2 small portions | **Prep time:** 5 minutes | **Creation time:** 15–20 minutes (5–8 minutes if you have a pre-cooked sweet potato)

2 cups (220 g) chopped sweet potato or yam, peeled

¼ cup (60 ml) full fat coconut milk

¼ tsp cinnamon to taste

2 pitted dates

2 tbsp (30 ml) vegan milk

1 tbsp (15 ml) maple syrup

1 tsp vanilla extract

¼ of a frozen banana

Boil the chopped sweet potato in a medium pot of water until tender, 12 to 15 minutes. This is the fastest way, but you are welcome to bake or boil the potatoes whole or however you prefer. Allow to cool.

Blend all of the ingredients together in a high-speed blender, adding more milk if it is too thick.

Chill at least 45 minutes before serving. Using a frozen banana will cut the time you will need to chill it.

PLAYFUL PB CHOCOLATE CHIP FROZEN *Dessert*

Banana, chocolate and peanut: one of the most delicious dessert combinations! High in slow-release energy and easy to make, this dessert will help you control your cravings for something sweet, while keeping you on track for healthy weight loss. Rich in monounsaturated fats, you'll also be supporting your heart, while the potassium boost from the banana will revitalize your blood.

Servings: 1 | **Prep time:** 2 minutes | **Creation time:** 8-10 minutes

1 frozen banana

2 tbsp (30 g) natural peanut butter, or sub almond butter or nut/seed butter of choice

1 tsp vanilla

Stevia to taste

2-4 tbsp (30-60 ml) of almond milk

1-2 tbsp (15-30 g) raw cacao nibs or vegan dark chocolate chips

Blend all of the ingredients, except the cacao nibs/chocolate chips, adding the almond milk a little bit at a time until the desired thickness has been reached.

Fold in the cacao nibs/chocolate chips and enjoy immediately.

WEEK 4

OVERVIEW

	MON	TUES	WED	THURS	FRI	SAT	SUN
BREAKFAST	Perfect Pear Smoothie	Coco-nana Smoothie	Beet This! Smoothie	Warrior-Worthy Smoothie	Blueberry Bonanza Smoothie	Feel Me Farro Bowl	Cajun Chickpea Fritters & Homemade Hazelnut Milk
LUNCH	Jammin' Jicama Apple Kale Salad	Luscious Leftovers	Healthful Hearts of Palm, Fennel & Farro Salad	Luscious Leftovers	Beautiful Beet & Quinoa Salad	Luscious Leftovers	
SNACK	Fresh Fruit of Choice	Fresh Fruit of Choice	Fresh Fruit of Choice	Fresh Fruit of Choice	Fresh Fruit of Choice	Fresh Fruit of Choice	Fresh Fruit of Choice
DINNER	Very Vegetable Soup & Herbed Chickpeas	Maple Baked Butternut Squash & Lemon Garlic Broccolini	Crave Me Cabbage Soup & Sautéed Beet Greens	Roasted Brussels Sprouts & Quinoa with Chickpeas & Sundried Tomatoes	Satiating Butternut Squash Soup & Mushroom Spinach Sauté	Sweet & Sour Tofu with Veggies	Fat Fighting Fajitas
TREAT	X	X	PB&J Balls	X	X	X	Just Peachy Sorbet
WORKOUT	Cross-Train (full body focus)	Cardio + Yoga	Cross-Train (upper body focus)	Cardio	Cross-Train (lower body focus)	Yoga + Cardio	Off/Rest

GROCERY LIST - WEEK 4

LIQUIDS

- Vegan milk of choice (40 oz [1.2 L])
- Coconut milk, culinary (1 tbsp [15 ml]) or full fat (1½ tbsp [24 ml])
- Coconut water (½ cup [120 ml])
- Vegetable broth (64 oz [1.9 L])

FRUIT

- Avocados (2)
- Apple (1)
- Bananas (3)
- Beets with greens (3)
- Lemon (½) or sub lemon juice
- Lime (½) or sub lime juice
- Orange, clementine/seedless (3)
- Pear (1)
- Pineapple chunks (½ cup [85 g])
- Frozen blueberries (1½ cups [230 g])
- Frozen peaches (2 cups [500 g])
- Frozen strawberries (5)
- Currants (1 cup [110 g]) or sub dates
- Dates (11)
- Golden raisins (½ cup [75 g])

LEAFY GREENS

- Arugula (2 handfuls)
- Baby spinach (9 handfuls)
- Kale, lacinato (not curly) (½–1 bunch)
- Romaine lettuce (1 cup [55 g], chopped)

VEGETABLES

- Beet (1)
- Bell pepper, green (2)
- Broccolini (1 bunch)
- Brussels sprouts (2 cups [195 g])
- Butternut squash (1)
- Cabbage, green (4 cups [360 g], chopped)
- Carrot (5)
- Celery (6 stalks/1 bunch)
- Cucumber (½)
- Endive (1 head)
- Fennel (1 bulb)
- Jicama (1)
- Mushrooms white or choice (½–1 package [8 oz (225 g)])
- Mushrooms, portobello cap (1 large)
- Onion, green (1 stalk)
- Onion, yellow (3)
- Radicchio (1 head)
- Summer squash (1)
- Sundried tomatoes (7)
- Sweet potato or yam (2)
- Tomato (1)
- Zucchini (2)
- Diced tomatoes (two 14.5-oz [410-g] cans)
- Tomato paste (one 6-oz [170-g] can)
- Hearts of palm (¾ cups [110 g])
- Fresh basil (1 tbsp [2.5 g])
- Fresh dill (<¼ oz [16 g])
- Fresh oregano (<¼ oz [16 g]) or sub dried
- Fresh curly parsley (1 cup [30 g])
- Garlic clove (1 bulb)

NUTS/SEEDS

- Hazelnuts (1 cup [115 g])
- Pecan pieces (¼ cup [30 g])
- Pine nuts (2 tbsp [18 g])
- Pistachios (2 tbsp [18 g]) or sub walnuts
- Walnuts (1½ cups [180 g])

LEGUMES

- Extra-firm tofu (1 lb [455 g])
- Black beans (½ cup [125 g])
- Chickpeas (two 15-oz [425-g] cans)
- Pinto beans (2¼ cans [15 oz (425 g)])

DRESSINGS/SAUCES/EXTRAS

- Cajun spice blend
- Chickpea flour (2 tbsp [30 g])

PREP DAY

- Cook quinoa
- Cook farro
- Chop vegetables for salads and soups
- Press tofu
- Bake butternut squash
- Cook sweet potatoes
- Steam beets

SUPER FOOD SMOOTHIE RECIPES

We will be recycling the smoothies from week one this week. Feel free to have some fun playing around with the ingredients, putting your own spin on the smoothies. You now have three weeks of experience to help you be creative with the recipes while keeping them healthy and in line with the Six Weeks to Sexy Abs Plan!

FEEL ME FARRO *Bowl*

Consider this a super-charged breakfast! Farro is an ancient whole grain with properties that regulate blood sugar, lower cholesterol and stimulate the immune system. With tons of slow-releasing energy, it will keep you shining until lunch, boosting your metabolism and spiking your nutrient levels to help you burn that fat faster. You can also count on the dried fruit for an extra vitamin boost.

Servings: 2 | **Prep time:** 5 minutes (does not include cooking the farro) | **Creation time:** 10 minutes

3 cups (555 g) cooked farro,* or sub quinoa

Splash of vegan milk

½ tsp cinnamon

1 heaping tbsp (15 g) flax meal

¼ cup (45 g) goji berries

¼ cup (30 g) walnut and/or pecan pieces

2 tbsp (14 g) almond slivers

Stevia powder to taste

OPTIONAL ADDITIONS

½ tbsp (7 g) vegan buttery spread

1 tbsp (15 ml) maple syrup

2 tbsp (30 g) unsweetened coconut flakes

Sliced strawberries and/or blueberries

Place the cooked farro, splash of milk and cinnamon in a small saucepan on the stove. Cook at medium-low heat and stir occasionally until hot—or use the microwave to heat.

Add the flax meal, goji berries, walnuts and/or pecans, almond slivers, optional additions and stevia to taste. Stir until thoroughly combined.

*Cooking farro: If there are instructions on the package, follow them. If not, rinse 1½ cups (260 g) farro well and then place in a medium saucepan with 4 cups (950 ml) of water (you can use vegetable broth for savory dishes) and ¼ teaspoon sea salt. Bring to a boil and then reduce heat to low and cook covered for around 30 minutes. The grain should be soft but still chewy. Drain excess water from the pot (if there is any); let it cool a few minutes and then "fluff" with a fork.

CAJUN CHICKPEA *Fritters* & HOMEMADE HAZELNUT *Milk*

A great source of that all-important protein and with a high amount of fiber and low GI (glycemic index), chickpeas make a great base for this brunch. Fritters are easy to make, filling and are paired perfectly with wilted spinach for a balanced, healthy meal. Hazelnuts make an awesome milk and are a good source of oleic acid, helping you to improve your cholesterol levels too. High in flavor, low in fat, enjoy!

CAJUN CHICKPEA FRITTERS

Servings: 2 | **Prep time:** 10 minutes | **Creation time:** 25–30 minutes

1 tbsp (15 ml) lemon juice

1 tbsp (15 g) tahini

1 cup (160 g) chopped onions

3 handfuls of spinach, divided

1 tbsp (12 g) nutritional yeast

2 garlic cloves, whole

½ tbsp (7 ml) extra virgin olive oil

1 tsp Cajun spice blend to taste

1½ cups (360 g) chickpeas, drained

1 zucchini, shredded

3–4 sundried tomatoes, diced

Sea salt and pepper to taste

A few dashes of hot sauce and/or cayenne pepper to taste

½ cup (60 g) chickpea flour

1 tsp avocado oil or sub coconut oil (refined)

1 garlic clove, minced

Combine the lemon juice, tahini, onions, 1 handful of the spinach, nutritional yeast, garlic, olive oil and spice, and mix in a high-speed blender—process until smooth.

Add the chickpeas, zucchini and sundried tomatoes to the blender, stir together and then slightly blend.

Add the sea salt and hot sauce or cayenne pepper to taste and enough chickpea flour as the mixture needs to create a thick batter consistency.

Heat a sauté pan with avocado oil to medium-high heat. Spoon enough of the batter into the pan to create about 2½-inch (6.4-cm) patties. Brown for 1 to 2 minutes on one side, flip and brown on the other side.

Once you've finished making the fritters, turn the heat down to medium; add a touch of olive oil and 1 clove of garlic, and sauté 1 minute. Add 2 handfuls of spinach and wilt. Serve alongside the fritters with salt and pepper to taste.

(continued)

HOMEMADE HAZELNUT MILK

Servings: 2 | **Prep time:** 12 hours of soaking the nuts | **Creation time:** 15 minutes

1 cup (135 g) raw hazelnuts, soaked 12+ hours

3–3½ cups (710–830 ml) water, depending how thick you like it

3-4 Medjool dates, pitted, soaking 30 minutes is recommended but not required

1 tsp pure vanilla extract

½ tsp cinnamon to taste

After soaking the hazelnuts at least 12 hours, drain and rinse them off.

Place all of the ingredients in a high-speed blender, work the speed to high and blend thoroughly.

Place a nut milk bag in a large bowl and pour the milk into it. Slowly strain the liquid through the bag by twisting and squeezing it until no more liquid will come out.

Fill your glass and keep the rest in a container tightly sealed in the fridge. It's best if you consume it within 2 days, but will last for about 3 days.

JAMMIN' JICAMA APPLE KALE *Salad*

Of Mexican origin, jicama is an amazing addition to the menu, because its fiber is infused with inulin, which contains no calories and promotes healthy intestines. Technically, jicama is in the legume family, but it has a texture and taste more like an apple or turnip. Jicama also promotes bone health, heart health and a balanced immune system to help keep your body in top condition.

This delicious salad is also packed full of one of the most nutrient-dense foods in the world: kale. The raisins provide an energy-boosting burst of sweetness. I suggest making a double portion, so you can use the whole jicama and have leftovers to eat during the rest of the week!

Servings: 1 lunch-size portion | **Prep time:** 15 minutes | **Creation time:** 10 minutes + 15 minutes allowing kale to soften

3 cups (200 g) chopped lacinato kale (not curly)

½ a lime, juiced

1 tbsp (15 ml) extra virgin olive oil

1 tbsp (15 ml) apple cider vinegar

⅛–¼ tsp sea salt to taste

Black pepper to taste

½ a jicama, peeled and cut into small cubes

1 carrot, shredded

2 tbsp (18 g) golden raisins

1 tbsp (4 g) chopped fresh dill

¼ cup (30 g) walnut halves

Place the chopped kale in a large bowl.

In a small bowl, whisk together the lime juice, olive oil, vinegar, sea salt and black pepper.

Pour the mixture over the kale and, using your hands, massage the dressing into the kale for several minutes.

Next add the jicama, carrots, raisins and dill, and mix thoroughly.

Allow the salad to sit for at least 15 minutes, preferably longer, to give the kale time to soften.

Mix the walnuts into the salad just before eating.

BEAUTIFUL BEET & QUINOA *Salad*

Beets are a highly nutritious root vegetable that play a role in improving cardiovascular health. They're also a brilliant color and make for a gorgeous salad! The quinoa adds complete protein and fills your tummy; the oranges add citrus sweetness and the pistachios add a perfect crunch to top it off!

Servings: 1 meal-size salad | **Prep time:** 10-15 minutes (not including cooking the quinoa) | **Creation time:** 20 minutes

3 beets, peeled and sliced

¾ cup (140 g) cooked cold quinoa

2 handfuls of arugula, chopped

1 stalk green onion, diced

1 clementine or other seedless orange, peeled and sectioned

2 tbsp (16 g) pistachios, or sub walnut pieces

DRESSING (OR USE SIMILAR STORE-BOUGHT VERSION)

4 tbsp (60 ml) extra virgin olive oil

3 tbsp (45 ml) red wine vinegar

½ tsp garlic powder

¼ tbsp (4 g) Dijon mustard

⅛ tsp ground black pepper

⅛ tsp sea salt to taste

Place a steamer insert into a saucepan, and fill the pan with water to just below the bottom of the steamer. Cover the pan and bring the water to a boil. Add the beets to the steamer, cover the pan and steam until the beets are just tender, 7 to 10 minutes. Set aside and allow to cool.

Whisk the dressing ingredients together in a small bowl.

In a larger bowl, combine the quinoa, chopped arugula, green onion, orange sections and beets.

Add 3 tablespoons (45 ml) of the dressing—the rest is to be stored in the fridge for another meal—and toss. To garnish, sprinkle the pistachios on top.

HEALTHFUL HEARTS OF PALM, FENNEL & FARRO *Salad*

As well as having an intriguing flavor similar to licorice, fennel has many health-promoting benefits, from reducing chronic inflammation to weight management and smoothing wrinkles. The farro will provide you with sustained energy and stop you from snacking—that plus the tasty dressing will leave you smacking your lips when you finish!

Servings: 1 lunch-size portion | **Prep time:** 10 minutes (not including cooking farro) | **Creation time:** 5–10 minutes

DRESSING (OR USE SIMILAR STORE-BOUGHT VARIATION)

1 tbsp (15 ml) extra virgin olive oil

1 tbsp (15 ml) red wine vinegar

1 tbsp (15 g) Dijon mustard

1 tbsp (15 ml) lemon juice

Touch of agave or a bit of date paste

¾ cup (140 g) cooked farro, or sub quinoa (gluten free)

1 fennel bulb, diced

1 head of endive, chopped

¾ cup (110 g) chopped hearts of palm

½ cup (65 g) orange slices

3 tbsp (24 g) walnut pieces

In a small bowl, whisk together the dressing ingredients.

In a large bowl, combine the farro, fennel, endive and hearts of palm, and then toss in the dressing. Place this all in a salad bowl, and add the orange slices and walnuts on top.

CRAVE ME CABBAGE *Soup* & SAUTÉED BEET GREENS

Cabbage makes a great high-nutrient, low-calorie soup base. Here it is complemented well with the protein and fiber of pinto beans and fantastic flavors of fresh herbs. For an even more filling meal, pair it with a side of beet greens. Many people buy beets for the bulb, not even realizing that the greens are actually the most nutrient dense part of the vegetable—and they're tasty when sautéed!

CRAVE ME CABBAGE SOUP

Servings: 3–4 large portions | Preparation time: 10 minutes | Creation time: 8 hours in the slow cooker

4 cups (360 g) chopped green cabbage

4 cups (950 ml) vegetable broth or water with vegetable bouillon cubes

1 (14.5 oz [410 g]) can diced tomatoes

1 tsp chili powder

2 tbsp (8 g) fresh, chopped oregano

2 celery stalks, chopped

1 carrot, shredded

1–2 tsp (5–10 ml) hot sauce to taste

¼ tsp garlic powder

¼ tsp salt to taste

Black pepper to taste

2 (15 oz [425 g]) cans pinto beans, drained and rinsed

Combine all of the ingredients in your slow cooker, and cook on low for 8 hours.

Taste and add more salt, pepper and/or hot sauce if needed.

SAUTÉED BEET GREENS

Servings: 1 | Prep time: 5–10 minutes | Creation time: 8–10 minutes

1 tsp sesame oil

1–2 cloves garlic, minced

2 cups (120 g) chopped beet greens

2–3 sundried tomatoes, diced, optional

Sea salt and pepper to taste

In a sauté pan set to medium-high, add the sesame oil and garlic and sauté for 30 seconds to 1 minute.

Add the beet greens and optional sundried tomatoes, a pinch of salt, and a bit of black pepper to the pan, and sauté until the greens are tender, about 5 to 7 minutes.

VERY VEGETABLE *Soup* & HERBED CHICKPEAS

Protect your body from a large array of diseases and fight fat with this immune-boosting dinner. Lovely for any time of day, this thick soup is packed with fibrous veggies in every mouthful. It freezes well and makes for a perfect, convenient meal when you otherwise may be tempted to place a delivery order! The herbed chickpeas are a perfect, quick side dish to increase the protein content of the meal.

This soup recipe involves quite a bit of vegetable chopping, so I recommend the slow cooker version because if you are like me, doing a bunch of chopping is enough work, and then I'm ready for the slow cooker to take over!

VERY VEGETABLE SOUP

Servings: 4 dinner-size servings | **Prep time:** 15-20 minutes | **Creation time:** 1 hour and 15 minutes using stovetop, or 8 hours using the slow cooker

2 tbsp (30 ml) extra virgin olive oil

2-3 garlic cloves, minced

1 onion, diced

3 carrots, diced

1 zucchini, chopped

1 yellow squash, chopped

3 stalks of celery, diced

1 (14.5 oz [410 g]) can diced tomatoes (salt free)

1 (6 oz [170 g]) can tomato paste

½ cup (30 g) curly parsley, chopped

4 cups (950 ml) vegetable broth

2 bay leaves

2 tsp (10 g) Italian seasoning

¼ tsp sea salt to taste

Black pepper to taste

1-2 tsp (5-10 ml) hot sauce to taste, optional

SLOW COOKER

Combine all of the ingredients in a slow cooker and cook on low for about 8 hours.

STOVETOP

Heat a large pot with olive oil to medium heat.

Place the garlic, onion and carrots in the pot and sauté for about 7 minutes before adding the zucchini, squash and celery. Sauté for about 8 to 10 minutes, until the veggies are fork tender.

Add the diced tomatoes, tomato paste, parsley, vegetable broth, bay leaves, Italian seasoning, sea salt, pepper and optional hot sauce to the pot.

Simmer covered for about an hour, and enjoy with a side of herbed chickpeas.

(continued)

HERBED CHICKPEAS

Servings: 3 side portions | **Prep time:** 5–8 minutes | **Creation time:** 2 minutes

1 (15 oz [425 g]) can chickpeas, drained and rinsed

1 tbsp (2.5 g) chopped fresh basil or 1 tsp dried basil

2 tbsp (8 g) chopped fresh parsley

1 tbsp (15 ml) fresh lemon juice

½ tbsp (7 ml) extra virgin olive oil

Sea salt and pepper to taste

Toss all of the ingredients together in a bowl, stir to coat the chickpeas and enjoy!

SATIATING BUTTERNUT SQUASH *Soup* & MUSHROOM SPINACH *Sauté*

Wow, this soup is phenomenal in every way! This is where prep day really comes into play to make this soup possible on a weekday. Just pop everything in the blender and you've got yourself a satiating soup with both sweetness and spice to address all types of cravings.

The mushrooms in the sauté provide the texture you need to totally satisfy you, and what would a meal be without the color green? This meal has it all!

SATIATING BUTTERNUT SQUASH SOUP

Servings: 2 | **Prep time:** 5 minutes if your potatoes and squash are pre-cooked, 45 minutes if they are not | **Creation time:** 5 minutes

2 small sweet potatoes, cooked

½ a butternut squash, roasted

1 tbsp (15 ml) culinary coconut milk or sub 1½ tbsp (24 ml) full fat coconut milk

¼ tsp curry powder

¼ tsp cinnamon

¼ tsp sea salt

Dash of nutmeg

1 cup (235 ml) vegan milk of choice

Dash of cayenne to taste

Black pepper to taste

Boil the sweet potatoes—if you do not have them already pre-cooked—for approximately 20 minutes until tender. Allow the potatoes to cool enough to handle, quarter them, place them in your high-speed blender and set aside.

If you do not have leftover baked butternut squash, preheat your oven to 375°F (190°C). Cut the squash in half lengthwise. Scoop out the seeds from the squash with a spoon and score the flesh with a fork. Place flesh-side down in a roasting pan and cook for 30 to 45 minutes or until you can stick a fork through the skin with some ease. The cooking time will depend largely on the size of the squash. For a convection oven, use 350°F (180°C) for about 30 minutes.

Combine all of the ingredients in your high-speed blender and process until smooth. Add more milk if needed for desired texture.

MUSHROOM SPINACH SAUTÉ

Servings: 1 | **Prep time:** 5 minutes | **Creation time:** 5 minutes

Touch of olive oil, or sub sesame oil

2 garlic cloves, chopped

2 cups (140 g) sliced white mushrooms or mushrooms of choice

3–4 sundried tomatoes, diced, optional

3 large handfuls spinach

2 tbsp (18 g) pine nuts

Sea salt and pepper to taste

Heat a large sauté pan with a touch of olive oil to medium heat. Add the garlic and sauté for about a minute, until just as it begins to brown.

Add the mushrooms and optional sundried tomatoes and sauté until they begin to become tender, about 4 to 6 minutes.

Add the spinach and pine nuts and stir constantly until the spinach leaves have wilted.

Remove from heat. Add salt and pepper to taste before serving.

MAPLE BAKED BUTTERNUT Squash & LEMON GARLIC BROCCOLINI

With its nutty flavor and mildly sweet taste, butternut squash is a great way to wind down from the day. The coconut, maple and cinnamon lend to the comfort you'll feel while eating this dish. If you roast double the amount of squash that will be served at dinner, you can save the leftover roasted squash to use for the Satiating Butternut Squash Soup (page 135) recipe.

Broccolini is rich in beneficial nutrients, among which include potassium and magnesium, both especially important for muscle growth and recovery.

MAPLE BAKED BUTTERNUT SQUASH

Servings: 2 | **Prep time:** 10 minutes | **Creation time:** 45–60 minutes

1 butternut squash, sliced in half lengthwise

1 tbsp (14 g) coconut oil (refined), melted (healthier) or sub vegan buttery spread

2 tbsp (30 ml) pure maple syrup

½ tsp cinnamon to taste

Sea salt to taste

¼ cup (28 g) pecans pieces

Preheat oven to 375°F (190°C).

Scoop out the seeds from the squash and score the flesh with a fork.

Place the two halves facedown in a roasting pan and in the oven. Cook for 30 to 45 minutes or until you can stick a fork through the skin with some ease. The cooking time will depend largely on the size of the squash. For a convection oven, use 350°F (180°C) for about 30 minutes.

Remove the squash halves from the oven and carefully flip the squash so the open sides are facing up.

In a small bowl, whisk together the coconut oil, maple syrup, cinnamon and salt. Spread the mixture over the flesh of the squash and then sprinkle the pecan pieces on top.

Return to the oven and cook for another 10 minutes.

Serve one half on a plate and eat by scooping out the flesh with a spoon.

LEMON GARLIC BROCCOLINI

Servings: 2 | **Prep time:** 5–8 minutes | **Creation time:** 12–15 minutes

1 bunch of broccolini, about 14 oz (400 g), trimmed

½ tbsp (7 ml) extra virgin olive oil

1 garlic clove, minced

Sea salt to taste

Black pepper to taste

Toasted pine nuts, optional

If you prefer a more tender vegetable, I recommend steaming the broccolini first, but this is an extra step that is not necessary.

Heat a skillet with olive oil to medium heat. Add the minced garlic and sauté for about 30 seconds.

Place the trimmed broccolini in the pan. Cook, stirring occasionally, until the broccolini stems are crisp tender, about 8 to 10 minutes. Add salt and pepper to taste and sauté for another 30 seconds.

If you are including the optional pine nuts, toast them in a single layer in the toaster oven until slightly browned.

Serve the broccolini, sprinkling the pine nuts on top just before eating so that they stay crunchy.

Roasted BRUSSELS SPROUTS & QUINOA WITH CHICKPEAS & SUNDRIED TOMATOES

This nutrient-filled meal exercises the power of simplicity. Brussels sprouts are high in iron and potassium, and quinoa is a good source of complete protein, so you'll receive a good mix of the essentials. Each dish has only five ingredients, allowing your taste buds to enjoy every crunchy, steamy, earthy element—while ensuring you have a short and easy preparation time! The quinoa side is great hot, or makes a great lunch leftover at room temperature as well.

ROASTED BRUSSELS SPROUTS

Servings: 1-2 | **Prep time:** 5 minutes | **Creation time:** 25-35 minutes

2 cups (175 g) Brussels sprouts, quartered or halved depending on size

¼ tsp sea salt to taste

Black pepper to taste

¼ cup (30 g) walnut pieces

1½-2 tbsp (24-30 ml) melted coconut oil (refined)

Preheat oven to 400°F (200°C).

Cut the Brussels sprouts into quarters, or halves if they are small and place them on a baking tray. Sprinkle sea salt and pepper over them and add the walnuts.

Drizzle the melted coconut oil over the Brussels sprouts and walnuts and bake for at least 20 to 30 minutes, until browned and slightly crispy.

QUINOA WITH CHICKPEAS & SUNDRIED TOMATOES

Servings: 2 side portions | **Prep time:** 8-10 minutes (not including cooking the quinoa) | **Creation time:** 5 minutes

½ cup (90 g) cooked quinoa

½ cup (120 g) chickpeas

2-3 sundried tomatoes, diced

1½ tbsp (6 g) chopped fresh parsley leaves

½ tbsp (7ml) extra virgin olive oil

Herbamare seasoning

Black pepper to taste

Place a saucepan over medium heat and add all of the ingredients to the pan.

Heat just until warm, about 5 minutes, stirring consistently.

*For instructions on how to cook quinoa, see page 44.

SWEET & SOUR *Tofu* WITH VEGGIES

This popular Chinese-style recipe will leave you feeling happy and healthy, rather than ordering take-out and feeling crappy! Sweet and sour sauce usually contains high amounts of processed sugar. I replaced the sugar with dates and pineapple so as to use only whole-food, nutritious ingredients. High in protein, vitamin C and potassium, this dish will continue to promote a healthy body while exciting the taste buds with an Asian-style meal.

Servings: 2 meal-size portions | **Prep time:** 10–15 minutes (+ 30 minutes soaking dates) | **Creation time:** 20 minutes

SAUCE (OR USE SIMILAR STORE-BOUGHT VERSION)

2 tbsp (30 ml) Bragg Liquid Aminos or tamari

4 tbsp (60 ml) rice vinegar, or sub apple cider vinegar

1 tbsp (15 g) ketchup

½ cup (80 g) pineapple

5 dates, pitted and soaked 30+ minutes

2–4 tbsp (30–60 ml) water

½–1 tbsp (7–14 g) coconut oil (refined)

1 lb (455 g) extra-firm tofu, drained and pressed*

1 medium onion, chopped

1 small green bell pepper, sliced

1 celery rib, chopped

2 cups (140 g) sliced cremini mushrooms or mushrooms of choice

1 cup (165 g) pineapple chunks

Prepare the sauce by combining all of the sauce ingredients together in a small saucepan. Use a muddler (my preference), fork or large spoon to mash the dates and pineapple. Place the saucepan on a burner set to medium heat. Cook, stirring regularly for about 5 minutes, then set aside.

Heat the coconut oil in a large skillet or wok to medium-high.

Stir-fry the tofu and onions for about 5 minutes. Then add the pepper and celery, sautéing for another 3 to 5 minutes—last add the mushrooms and pineapple.

When the mushrooms begin to soften, 3–5 minutes, add the sauce and continue to sauté for a couple minutes until the vegetables are all tender.

*See page 43 for instructions on pressing tofu.

FAT FIGHTING *Fajitas*

Fajitas are a popular, fun-to-eat meal, and with this recipe, you also receive great health benefits! You'll enjoy a ton of protein and fiber from the beans and a vitamin boost from the veggies. And even though avocados are high in fat (good fat), they can actually promote a healthy BMI (body mass index) and help lower bad cholesterol levels. With a touch of spice and a spoonful of salsa on top, you'll finish your plate well satisfied! They're also great for sharing!

Servings: 2–3 meal-size portions | **Prep time:** 15 minutes | **Creation time:** 20 minutes

Dash of avocado oil, or sub grape seed oil

1 cup (160 g) onion, chopped

1 cup (150 g) sliced bell pepper(s) of choice

1 large (or 2 small) portobello mushroom caps, sliced

¼ tsp black pepper

½ cup (125 g) black beans, drained and rinsed

½ cup (125 g) pinto beans, drained and rinsed

Taco seasoning to taste, optional

Hot sauce to taste, optional

Radicchio leaves

¼ cup (30 g) Daiya pepper jack shreds, optional

1 cup (55 g) romaine lettuce, shredded

1 cup (180 g) diced fresh tomatoes

1 avocado, sliced

Salsa to taste

Heat a skillet with oil to medium-high.

Sauté the onions until they become translucent.

Add the peppers, mushrooms and black pepper, and continue to sauté until slightly browned, about 6 to 8 minutes.

Meanwhile, heat the beans with optional taco seasoning and hot sauce in a small saucepan on medium-low, stirring occasionally so they don't stick to the bottom, or heat them in the microwave.

To serve, spoon some beans and sauté mix into a radicchio leaf.

If you choose to use Daiya shreds, sprinkle them over the hot mix so they will melt.

Next, add the shredded lettuce, tomatoes, avocado and salsa to taste.

JUST PEACHY *Sorbet*

With a full and rich flavor, peach sorbet makes a great, virtually fat-free dessert option. It also has only three ingredients and takes less than 10 minutes to make, start to finish. Now that's what I call peachy!

Servings: 2 | **Prep time:** 2 minutes | **Creation time:** 5 minutes

2 cups (500 g) frozen peach slices

1 small frozen banana

3–5 tbsp (45–75 ml) almond milk, as needed

Combine all of the ingredients in a high-speed blender and process until smooth and creamy, using just enough almond milk to allow for blending. Serve immediately.

PB&J Balls

A mouthwatering sweet snack that's rich in monounsaturated fats and a good source of antioxidants. Did you know that peanuts are actually classified as legumes? Like other legumes, peanuts reduce the risk of coronary heart disease, and it's been found that frequent legume eaters are less likely to gain weight in comparison to those who eat legumes less regularly. If you have peanut allergies, or you just want to change it up, try using almond butter or any type of nut or seed butter you enjoy.

Servings: 3 | **Prep time:** 5 minutes | **Creation time:** 10 minutes + 15 minutes to chill in freezer

---

¾ cup (60 g) rolled oats

1 cup (175 g) dried currants or pitted dates

½ cup (130 g) peanut butter, or sub almond butter or nut/seed butter of choice

1½ tsp (7 ml) vanilla extract

½ tsp ground cinnamon

OPTIONAL ADDITIONS

½ tbsp (7 g) sesame seeds

Place ingredients in a food processor and process until well-blended and sticky.

Scoop out one spoonful at a time and roll into a ball in your palms.

Chill balls in the freezer or refrigerator until firm, about 15 minutes, before eating.

WEEK 5

OVERVIEW

	MON	TUES	WED	THURS	FRI	SAT	SUN
BREAKFAST	Orange-sicle Smoothie	Chocolate Brazil Booty Smoothie	Basil Strawberryita Smoothie	Banana Bread Smoothie	Awesome Acai Smoothie	Berry Granola Parfait	TKO Tofu Omelet & Sweet Potato Hash
LUNCH	Lusty Lentil Mint Salad	Luscious Leftovers	Beyond Grilled Chicken Caesar Salad	Luscious Leftovers	Radicchio, Pear & Walnut Salad	Luscious Leftovers	
SNACK	Fresh Fruit of Choice	Fresh Fruit of Choice	Fresh Fruit of Choice	Fresh Fruit of Choice	Fresh Fruit of Choice	Fresh Fruit of Choice	Fresh Fruit of Choice
DINNER	Tummy Tuck Tomato Soup & Garlic Hummus	Not-So-Naughty Noodle & Veggie Stir Fry	Love-Me-Lentil Soup & Fresh Basil Tomatoes	Rosemary Romance Stuffed Mushrooms & Sweet Summer Corn on the Cob	Sweet Potato, Kale & Chickpea Soup	Rockin' Roots and Tofu	Not Yo' Mama's Black-Eyed Peas and Collard Greens
TREAT	X	X	Anna Banana Strawberry Delight	X	X	X	Nutella-Inspired Mousse
WORKOUT	Cross-Train (full body focus)	Cardio + Yoga	Cross-Train (upper body focus)	Cardio	Cross-Train (lower body focus)	Yoga + Cardio	Off/Rest

GROCERY LIST - WEEK 5

LIQUIDS

- Vegan milk (32 oz [950 ml])
- Coconut water (26 oz [770 ml])
- Coconut milk, full fat (¼ cup [60 ml])
- Vegetable broth (80 oz [2.4 L])

FRUIT

- Avocados (1½)
- Bananas (6)
- Berries of choice (1½ cups [185 g])
- Lemons (2)
- Oranges (2 large)
- Frozen acai (1 cup [65 g])
- Frozen blueberries (½ cup [125 g])
- Frozen strawberries (2½ cups [640 g])
- Dates (10)

LEAFY GREENS

- Arugula (2 cups [40 g])
- Baby spinach (2 handfuls)
- Kale, lacinato (<1 bunch)
- Romaine hearts (4 cups [225 g], chopped)

VEGETABLES

- Beets (2)
- Bell pepper, green (½)
- Bell pepper, red (1)
- Broccoli florets (2–3 cups [140–210 g])
- Carrots (5 cups [650 g])
- Celery (1 cup [100 g])
- Cherry tomatoes (two 10.5-oz [300-g] containers)
- Collard greens (½ a bunch)
- Cucumber (½)
- Mushrooms, white (two 8-oz [225-g] packages)
- Parsnip (1)
- Onion, green (1 stalk)
- Onion, yellow (2 large)
- Radicchio (2 cups [235 g], chopped)
- Summer corn on the cob (1 ear)
- Sweet potato or yam (3)
- Tomato (½)
- Turnip (1)
- Whole peeled tomatoes (one 14.5-oz [410-g] can or 3 fresh tomatoes blanched)
- Tomato paste (one 6-oz [170-g] can)
- Fresh basil (¼ oz [7 g])
- Fresh mint leaves (½ oz [15 g])
- Fresh oregano leaves (<¼ oz [15 g]) or sub dried
- Fresh parsley (½ cup [30 g])
- Fresh rosemary leaves (1 tbsp [1.7 g])
- Fresh thyme (1 tbsp [2.4 g]) or sub dried
- Garlic cloves (½ a bulb)

NUTS/SEEDS

- Brazil nuts (8)
- Cashews (⅓ cup [50 g])
- Hazelnut butter (2 tbsp [30 g]) or sub nut butter of choice
- Walnuts (½ cup [75 g])

LEGUMES

- Extra-firm tofu (1 lb [455 g])
- Silken tofu (1 lb [455 g])
- Beyond Meat Grilled Chicken free strips (8)
- Tempeh bacon (a few strips) or Bac'Un bits
- Black-eyed peas (one 15-oz [425-g] can)
- Cannellini beans (one 15-oz [425-g] can)
- Chickpeas (one 15-oz [425-g] can)
- Lentils (3½ 15-oz [425-g] cans)

VEGAN DAIRY

- Vegan yogurt, plain unsweetened (1½ cups [345 g])

WHOLE GRAINS

- Granola, fruit sweetened (¼ cup [50 g])
- Whole grain croutons (½ cup [60 g])

DRESSINGS/SAUCES/EXTRAS

- Chickpea flour (3 tbsp [45 g])
- Explore Asian Edamame & Mung Bean Fettuccini or Adzuki Bean Spaghetti (½ a package)
- Hummus (store-bought) or add chickpeas (one 15-oz [425-g] can)
- Ginger stir-fry sauce, store-bought or add fresh ginger (1 tbsp [6 g], minced)

PREP DAY

- Cook quinoa
- Chop vegetables for salads, soups, and stir fry
- Press tofu

SUPER FOOD SMOOTHIE RECIPES

We will be recycling the smoothies from week two this week. Feel free to have some fun playing around with the ingredients, putting your own spin on the smoothies. You now have four weeks of experience to help you be creative with the recipes while keeping them healthy and in line with the Six Weeks to Sexy Abs Plan!

BERRY GRANOLA *Parfait*

This breakfast is colorful, sweet and filled with interesting textures. Your bowl will be brimming with omega-3 fatty acids, vitamin C and healthy nut proteins, all speeding up your body's ability to burn fat and giving it muscle-building fuel. You don't need to be afraid to have what you crave when it comes to this recipe.

Servings: 1 | **Prep time:** 5 minutes | **Creation time:** 5 minutes

1 cup (230 g) vegan yogurt, plain and unsweetened

1½ cups (220 g) fresh blueberries, raspberries and/or sliced strawberries

¼ cup (40 g) fruit-sweetened granola, free from refined sugars

2 tbsp (14 g) coconut flakes

1 tbsp (9 g) goji berries, optional

1 tbsp (8 g) hemp seeds, optional

Place ingredients in your bowl in the order listed and enjoy!

TKO TOFU OMELET & SWEET POTATO *Hash*

This brunch is a protein-packed knock out! Omelets are such a popular brunch favorite, and now you can enjoy them while sticking to your meal plan! As a bonus, this tofu omelet recipe is quick and simple to prepare.

TKO TOFU OMELET

Servings: 2 large omelets | **Prep time:** 5–8 minutes | **Creation time:** 15 minutes

2 tsp (10 g) coconut oil (refined)

OMELET BATTER

1 package (1 lb [455 g]) silken tofu (firm or extra-firm), drained

3 tbsp (45 g) chickpea flour

½ tbsp (4 g) cornstarch

1 tbsp (12 g) nutritional yeast

½ tsp turmeric

¼ tsp onion granules or powder

1 tsp Herbamare seasoning

FILLING

1½ cups (100 g) sliced white button mushrooms

1 handful of baby spinach

½ cup (90 g) fresh, diced tomato

Daiya shreds, optional

Black pepper to taste

In your high-speed blender, combine the omelet batter ingredients and process until smooth.

Heat two skillets or frying pans, each with a teaspoon of coconut oil, to medium-high.

In one skillet, place the mushrooms and sauté, adding the spinach and tomatoes once the mushrooms begin to soften. Turn off the heat when the spinach has wilted.

In the other skillet, pour the omelet batter into the pan. Tilt the pan using the handle and move it in circular motions to spread the batter out until it is a thin layer on the pan. Use a spatula around the outer edges to form a circle.

Be patient and wait until the bottom has browned and the batter has become solid enough all the way through to flip. You may need to turn the heat down a bit in the process.

Flip and sprinkle some Daiya shreds (optional) and black pepper to taste

Brown the second side, making sure the batter has cooked all the way through.

Add some filling to one side of the omelet, fold the omelet over the filling using your spatula and serve.

SWEET POTATO HASH

Servings: 2 | **Prep time:** 10 minutes | **Creation time:** 15 minutes

½ tbsp (7 g) refined coconut oil

1 sweet potato or yam, peeled, grated

½ tsp cinnamon

Sea salt to taste

Heat a skillet with refined coconut oil to medium-high heat.

Toss the grated sweet potato with the cinnamon and salt. Spread the sweet potatoes out into a thin layer on the heated skillet and allow to cook until browned, about 5 to 7 minutes. Flip and allow the second side to brown.

LUSTY LENTIL MINT *Salad*

Full of tasty greens and packed full of highly nutritious lentils, this salad is a clean and refreshing choice. Fresh pops of sweet cherry tomatoes give the salad a variety of textures. It's quick to make and the fresh herbs coupled with zingy lemon will perk up your taste buds too.

Servings: 2 meal-size salads | **Prep time:** 15 minutes | **Creation time:** 10 minutes

2 cups (135 g) finely chopped lacinato kale (not curly), stems removed

2 tbsp (30 ml) extra virgin olive oil, divided

1 can (15 oz [425 g]) lentils, drained and rinsed

1 green onion, diced

½ a red pepper, diced

12–15 grape or cherry tomatoes, quartered

⅓ of a medium cucumber, diced

¼ cup (24 g) loosely packed mint leaves, chopped

¼ cup (15 g) loosely packed curly parsley, chopped

½ a large lemon, juiced

¼ tsp sea salt

Place the kale in a large bowl and add 1 tablespoon (15 ml) of olive oil. Using your hands, massage the kale with the olive oil to coat and tenderize the leaves.

Add the rest of the ingredients, and toss thoroughly.

This salad is best if allowed to sit in fridge for a few hours, or until the next day, to allow the kale time to become tender, but it can be eaten right away as well.

RADDICCHIO, PEAR & WALNUT *Salad*

Sweet, nutty and sharp flavors combine to tickle your taste buds while boosting your health. The fruits will give you immediate energy and the nuts will provide time-released energy, so you will be set to take on the rest of the afternoon.

Servings: 1 lunch-size salad with 1+ extra portions of dressing | **Prep time:** 10 minutes | **Creation time:** 5–10 minutes

DRESSING (OR USE STORE-BOUGHT BALSAMIC SALAD DRESSING)

4 tbsp (60 ml) extra virgin olive oil

2 tbsp (30 ml) balsamic vinegar

1 tsp Dijon mustard

¼ tsp garlic powder

1 tsp agave nectar, or sub date paste

Sea salt and pepper to taste

2 cups (110 g) chopped radicchio

2 cups (40 g) arugula (about one large handful)

1 cup (55 g) sliced pear

½ a small avocado, sliced

¼ cup (30 g) walnut pieces

Whisk together the dressing ingredients.

Combine the radicchio and arugula in a large bowl and toss with 1 tablespoon (15 ml) of the dressing.

Add the pear, avocado and walnuts, in that order, on top of the greens. Drizzle with another tablespoon (15 ml) of dressing. Store the rest of the dressing in a sealed container in the fridge.

BEYOND GRILLED CHICKEN CAESAR *Salad*

If Caesar salad is on your list of favorites, this one is for you! Crisp romaine hearts sit alongside crunchy croutons and delicious Beyond Meat's Beyond Chicken Grilled Strips. It's quick to prepare, high in protein and made extra special with this tasty Caesar dressing recipe.

Servings: 1 meal-size salad with 1 extra portion of dressing | **Prep time:** 5-10 minutes | **Creation time:** 10 minutes

---

4-5 Beyond Meat Grilled Chicken Strips

Drop of avocado oil, or sub grape seed oil

¼ cup (30 g) vegan, whole grain croutons

4 cups (225 g) chopped romaine hearts

½ cup (60 g) sliced cucumber, optional

½ cup (90 g) chopped tomato, optional

¼ of an avocado, sliced

DRESSING (OR USE STORE-BOUGHT VEGAN CAESAR SALAD DRESSING)

2 tbsp (28 g) vegan mayonnaise

1 tbsp (15 ml) extra virgin olive oil

½ tbsp (7 ml) fresh lemon juice

¼-½ tsp vegan Worcestershire sauce

Sea salt and pepper to taste

Cook the Beyond Meat Chicken Strips in a frying pan with oil on medium-high until they are slightly browned on both sides, about 6 to 8 minutes.

Toast the croutons in the toaster oven on 350°F (180°C) until slightly browned, about 4 minutes.

In a small bowl, whisk together the dressing ingredients.

Place the romaine lettuce, optional cucumber and tomato in a large bowl and toss with 1 tablespoon (15 ml) of the dressing. Add the chicken strips—you can either leave them whole and cut them as you eat, or cut them before putting them in the salad—and avocado slices on top of the lettuce.

Drizzle another ½-1 tablespoon (7-15 ml) of dressing over the salad. Store the rest of the dressing in a sealed container in the fridge.

Add the croutons last so they stay crunchy.

TUMMY TUCK TOMATO *Soup* AND GARLIC *Hummus*

Go ahead and make this big batch of delectable soup! Creamy, satisfying and filling, this soup goes well with almost any side dish or simply some whole grain crackers. It's a classic that also happens to be outstanding in terms of heart health and free of bad calories to help you achieve the shape you want.

Hummus with veggies is a great "go-to" side for any soup. You can either use this recipe for homemade hummus—it's quick and easy—or buy premade hummus at the store. If you go with store-bought hummus, make sure to read the nutrition label to make sure it's "clean" with only whole-food ingredients and no added junk!

TUMMY TUCK TOMATO SOUP

Servings: 2 large portions | **Prep time:** 8–10 minutes using canned tomatoes, 15–20 minutes using fresh (not including 4 hours soaking the cashews) | **Creation time:** 20 minutes

⅓ cup (35 g) cashews, soaked

⅓ cup (78 ml) water

½ of a small yellow onion, chopped

2 garlic cloves, diced

1 tbsp (14 g) refined coconut oil, refined

1 (14.5 oz [410 g]) can whole peeled tomatoes or 3 large tomatoes, blanched*

1 (6 oz [170 g]) can tomato paste

1 tbsp (4 g) chopped fresh oregano leaves or 1 tsp dried

1 tbsp (2.4 g) fresh thyme leaves or 1 tsp dried

1 tbsp (15 ml) balsamic vinegar

¼ cup (60 ml) coconut milk, full fat

¼ tsp sea salt to taste

A few dashes of hot sauce to taste

Black pepper to taste

Soak the cashews at least 4 hours, then blend with the water and set aside.

In a pan, sauté the onion and garlic in 1 tablespoon (15 ml) of coconut oil until they become translucent and tender.

In a large pot, combine the onion and garlic with all of the other ingredients and blend together using an immersion blender.

Cook for 10 minutes on medium-low, stirring occasionally, until the soup is hot.

*To blanch tomatoes, boil a large pot of water. Carve a small "x" in the bottom of the tomatoes and place them in the water. Once the skin starts to peel off, about 30 seconds, remove the tomatoes and place them in a large bowl of ice water. Once cooled, remove the skins completely. Whole peeled canned tomatoes can be substituted as a convenient alternative.

(continued)

GARLIC HUMMUS

Servings: 4 side/snack-size portions | **Prep time:** 5 minutes | **Creation time:** 5–10 minutes

3 cloves garlic, minced

1 tbsp (15 ml) extra virgin olive oil

1 (15 oz [425 g]) can chickpeas, drained and rinsed

½ a large lemon, juiced

1 tbsp (15 g) tahini

¼–½ tsp sea salt to taste

Raw vegetables, for serving

Sauté the fresh garlic with olive oil for 1–2 minutes in a small skillet on medium heat.

Process the garlic with all of the other ingredients in a food processor, high-speed blender or using an immersion blender until smooth.

Serve with either raw vegetables (celery, cucumber, carrots, etc.), which will be most helpful aiding weight loss, or whole grain/seed crackers.

LOVE-ME-LENTIL *Soup* & FRESH BASIL TOMATOES

This delicious soup is super filling, so a simple side of herbed tomatoes makes the perfect accompaniment. This tasty, high-fiber meal is great for your heart. Lentils also provide solid protein and will help you keep a lid on cravings for snacks.

This soup freezes well so you may want to double up on the batch and freeze half to have a convenient meal at some point down the road. You have the option to use the stovetop or slow cooker for this one. Either way it will turn out great!

LOVE-ME-LENTIL SOUP

Servings: 3 | **Prep time:** 15 minutes | **Creation time:** 40 minutes using the stovetop option, or 8 hours in the slow cooker

1 tbsp (15 ml) extra virgin olive oil

1 cup (160 g) diced onion

3 cloves fresh garlic, minced or 1 tbsp (10 g) bottled minced garlic

1 cup (130 g) thinly sliced carrots

¾ cup (125 g) diced green pepper

1 cup (100 g) chopped celery

1½ cups (100 g) sliced mushrooms

4–5 cups (945–1180 ml) vegetable broth

½ cup (35 g) chopped kale or 1 cup (30 g) baby spinach

2 tsp (2 g) dried oregano

2½ cups (480 g) canned lentils, sodium free

¼ tsp sea salt to taste

Black pepper to taste

STOVETOP

Heat a large pot with the olive oil to medium heat. Add the onions and garlic and sauté for about a minute.

Add the carrots, peppers and celery and continue to sauté for about 8 to 10 minutes.

When the carrots become flexible, add the mushrooms.

When the mushrooms begin to soften, add the vegetable broth (4 cups [945 ml] for thicker soup, 5 cups [1180 ml] for thinner soup), kale, oregano, lentils, sea salt and pepper, and bring to a boil.

Reduce the heat and simmer for 20 to 30 minutes.

SLOW COOKER

Place all of the ingredients in the slow cooker. Cook on the low setting around 8 hours.

If you prefer the lentils to be firm, you can add them when there is only 1 hour left to cook, or substitute the canned lentils for 1 cup (190 g) of dry lentils and put them in at the beginning.

FRESH BASIL TOMATOES

Servings: 2 side portions | **Prep time:** 5 minutes | **Creation time:** 2 minutes

2 cups (300 g) cherry or grape tomatoes

½ tbsp (7 ml) extra virgin olive oil

1 tbsp (2.5 g) chopped fresh basil, or sub 1 tsp dried basil

Sea salt to taste

Cracked black pepper to taste

Cut the tomatoes in half crosswise and place them in a bowl.

Toss in the olive oil, basil, salt and pepper.

SWEET POTATO, KALE & CHICKPEA *Soup*

This slow-cooker soup is both sweet and savory to ensure your satisfaction. Thick and bursting with flavor, vitamins, minerals and fiber, it's a perfect end to a long day. Sweet potatoes, kale and chickpeas are all heavyweights when it comes to fighting for a lean, healthy body.

Servings: 4 | **Prep time:** 15 minutes | **Creation time:** 8 hours in the slow cooker + 10 minutes active kitchen time

2 medium-size sweet potatoes, chopped

2 cups (135 g) chopped kale leaves

1 (15 oz [425 g]) can chickpeas, drained and rinsed

4 cups (945 ml) vegetable broth

¼ cup (15 g) chopped parsley

1 tsp cinnamon

¼ tsp turmeric

Dash of nutmeg (less than ⅛ tsp)

1 tsp cumin

⅛ tsp cayenne, plus more to taste

½ tsp sea salt to taste

2 tbsp (30 ml) extra virgin olive oil

Combine all of the ingredients in a slow cooker. Cook on low for 8 to 10 hours.

Use an immersion blender to process the soup until smooth. Taste and add more sea salt and/or cayenne to taste.

NOT-SO-NAUGHTY NOODLE & VEGGIE Stir Fry

Most types of noodles don't do a body good. These noodles on the other hand have a surprising 25 grams of protein and 17 grams of fiber in every serving! A pasta that supports weight loss! In this case, we are using the mung bean fettuccini as a substitute for lo mein, rice or soba noodles. Stir-fried vegetables add a nice crunch, and the gingery sauce boosts your body's health and is soothing to your stomach. Either chop fresh veggies or buy a frozen, pre-chopped blend to save you time and energy. Top it off with sesame seeds as a finishing touch.

Servings: 2 | **Prep time:** 15 minutes (less if you used precut veggies and/or premade sauce) | **Creation time:** 15–20 minutes

SAUCE (OR USE STORE-BOUGHT GINGER STIR FRY SAUCE)

¼ cup (60 ml) Bragg Liquid Aminos

1 tbsp (15 ml) sesame oil

1½ tbsp (24 g) tahini

1 tbsp (6 g) minced ginger or ½–1 tsp ginger powder

¼–½ tsp garlic powder

½ tsp cornstarch

Dash of red pepper or chili pepper flakes to taste, optional

½ a package of Explore Asia Edamame & Mung Bean Fettuccini or Adzuki Bean Spaghetti

2 tbsp (16 g) sesame seeds

VEGETABLES (OR USE A PRECUT FROZEN MIX)

½–1 tbsp (7–15 ml) sesame oil

2 cloves garlic, minced

1 cup (160 g) diced yellow onion

1 small head of broccoli, chopped into small florets

1 carrot, julienned

1 cup (150 g) sliced red bell pepper

2 cups (140 g) sliced mushrooms

In a small bowl, whisk together the sauce ingredients and set aside.

Bring a large pot of water to boil and add the pasta. Reduce heat and cook at a rolling boil for 5 to 7 minutes. Drain and set aside.

Meanwhile, heat a sauté pan with sesame oil to medium/medium-high heat. Add the garlic and yellow onion and sauté for a few minutes.

Add the vegetables in the following order: broccoli (sauté another couple minutes), carrots and red pepper (sauté another couple minutes), then mushrooms last when the other veggies are starting to become tender.

Once the mushrooms begin to soften, push the vegetables to the edges of the pan with your spatula and pour the sauce in the middle. Stir it around the center of the pan as it thickens. Then mix the sauce in with the vegetables and finish cooking until all of the vegetables have reached the desired tenderness.

Add noodles and sesame seeds to the vegetables and sauté until thoroughly mixed and hot, about 3 to 4 minutes.

ROSEMARY ROMANCE STUFFED *Mushrooms* & SWEET SUMMER CORN ON THE COBB

Rosemary provides an alluring aromatic touch to any meal. With antioxidant properties and essential oils, it's super healthy as well as super delicious! Mushrooms provide more nutrition and health benefits than we once thought. Surprisingly quick to prepare, this dish appears stylish on a plate and is the perfect way to impress a guest without laboring in the kitchen for long! What can I say about the corn on the cob side, except, "Who doesn't like corn on the cob?!"

ROSEMARY ROMANCE STUFFED MUSHROOMS

Servings: 2 | **Prep time:** 10 minutes | **Creation time:** 30 minutes

10-12 large white mushrooms

2-3 cloves garlic, minced

1 tbsp (15 ml) extra virgin olive oil

1 (15 oz [425 g]) can cannellini beans (no salt added)

1 lemon, juiced, or sub 2 tbsp (30 ml) lemon juice

1 tbsp (1.7 g) fresh rosemary leaves

1 tbsp (15 g) tahini

¼ tsp sea salt

Dash of cayenne to taste

2 tbsp (30 ml) water

Black pepper to taste

½-1 tbsp (1.5-3 g) dried chives

Preheat the oven to 375°F (190°C).

Wipe the mushrooms clean with a damp paper towel. Carefully separate the stems from the mushrooms. Cut off the tough bottom section of the stems and throw the tough part away. Then, finely chop what's left of the stems.

Sauté the stems and garlic in 1 tablespoon (15 ml) of olive oil in a sauté pan on medium heat for 3 to 5 minutes until stems are tender and garlic is golden brown.

Process the beans, lemon juice, rosemary, tahini, salt, cayenne, water and black pepper in a food processor until smooth and creamy. Add more water if necessary.

Transfer the blended bean mix to a mixing bowl, and add the mushroom stem and garlic sauté mix, stirring until thoroughly combined.

Grease the bottom of a cooking sheet with a touch of olive oil or olive oil spray, and place the mushrooms, caps down, on the sheet.

Spoon the stuffing into each cap. Sprinkle with the chives.

Bake for about 15 minutes or until mushrooms are tender and juicy.

SWEET SUMMER CORN ON THE COBB

Servings: 1 | **Prep time:** 5 minutes | **Creation time:** 10 minutes

1 ear of fresh corn, husked

Earth Balance Buttery spread or EVOO to taste

Fresh cracked pepper to taste

½ tsp sea salt

If the ear of corn is too large to fit in a pot, cut it in half.

Bring a large pot of water with the sea salt to boil.

Add the corn and return to a boil. Reduce heat and cook at a rolling boil for 5 to 7 minutes, or until corn is tender.

Carefully remove the corn from the water.

Spread a thin layer of buttery spread or olive oil onto the corn, and add fresh cracked black pepper and sea salt to taste.

NOT YO' MAMA'S BLACK-EYED *Peas* AND COLLARD GREENS

Coming from North Carolina, I had to throw in a healthy version of a good ol' Southern-style dish! This is certainly one. Collard greens are exceptionally helpful at lowering cholesterol, reducing oxidative stress to our cells and have a detoxifying effect on our digestive system. Combined with the incredibly high fiber content of black-eyed peas and the flavor of bacon, this is a dinner winner!

For a more filling meal with even more protein, use the tempeh bacon option. Otherwise, just stick with some Bac'Uns and count on the beans to do enough tummy filling to last you the night.

Servings: 2 | **Prep time:** 5–10 minutes | **Creation time:** 15 minutes

2 garlic cloves, minced

1½ tbsp (24 ml) olive oil

2 cups (475 ml) vegetable stock

1–2 tbsp (15–30 g) vegan bacon bits* to taste or tempeh bacon, cooked according to directions on package

2 tbsp (30 ml) vegan Worcestershire sauce

½ a bunch of collard greens, chopped

1 (15 oz [425 g]) can black-eyed peas

Sea salt and pepper to taste

Sauté the garlic in the olive oil over medium heat.

Add the vegetable stock, bacon bits and Worcestershire sauce, and stir.

Add collard greens and cook for about 5 minutes or until tender.

Add the black-eyed peas, stir and cook until hot. If you are using tempeh bacon, you can simply add it at the end. Salt and pepper to taste.

*Recommended brands: Frontier Bac'Uns, Lightlife Fakin' Bacon

ROCKIN' *Roots* AND TOFU

This dish has an earthy sweetness that's delicious and fulfilling. It has plenty of protein from the tofu, and the root vegetables are loaded with vitamin C and folate. This is one dish with quite a bit of chopping prep time, but you will end up with plenty of leftovers to save you time the rest of the week.

Servings: 4 | **Prep time:** 15–20 minutes | **Creation time:** 40 minutes

TOFU MARINADE (OR USE A SIMILAR STORE-BOUGHT VERSION)

4 tbsp (60 ml) olive oil

4 tbsp (60 g) tamari or Bragg Liquid Aminos (60 ml)

½ tbsp (7 ml) spicy brown mustard

1 tbsp (12 g) nutritional yeast

1 tsp cornstarch

1 (1 lb [455 g]) block extra-firm tofu, drained, pressed*, and cut into ¾" (2 cm) cubes

3 carrots, chopped

2 beets, chopped

1 turnip, chopped

1 parsnip, chopped

1 small yellow onion

1–2 tsp (5–10 g) coconut oil, refined

3–4 tbsp (45–60 ml) balsamic vinegar

Sea salt and black pepper to taste

Preheat oven to 450°F (230°C).

Whisk together the marinade ingredients in a small bowl.

Add the tofu cubes to the marinade and stir so that all the tofu is covered with the marinade. Let this soak for at least 10 minutes.

Meanwhile, chop the vegetables into bite-size chunks and place in large bowl.

Pour the marinade from the tofu over the vegetables and toss to coat.

Grease 2 baking pans with coconut oil.

Place the vegetables on one baking pan and the tofu on the other, both in a single layer.

Place the trays in the oven and bake for about 15 minutes until vegetables and tofu start to brown.

Remove from the oven and drizzle balsamic vinegar over the vegetables and tofu, mixing them around and spreading them out into a single layer again.

Put back in oven for another 10 to 15 minutes. Remove and add sea salt and black pepper to taste.

*See page 43 for instructions for pressing tofu.

ANNA BANANA STRAWBERRY *Delight*

This incredible dessert, originally created by my creative, beautiful sister Anna, couldn't be quicker or easier to make. No prep work! It's the answer to an after-dinner craving for a sweet treat.

Servings: 2 | **Prep time:** 2 minutes | **Creation time:** 5 minutes

---

1 large frozen banana

1 cup (255 g) frozen strawberries

Splash of almond milk

Pecan pieces, optional

Blend all of the ingredients, except the pecan pieces, in a high-speed blender. Start with just a splash of almond milk and add a little bit at a time until the desired thickness has been reached.

Sprinkle the pecan pieces on top if you'd like a little crunch.

NUTELLA-INSPIRED *Mousse*

The texture, versatility and incredibly healthy flesh of avocados gives the perfect creaminess to this irresistible mousse. Rich in healthy fatty acids, with high levels of antioxidants and digestion-aiding properties from the dates, it's a great way to finish off your day. Make sure to soak the dates at least 30 minutes before you're ready to whip up this treat. If you freeze the almond milk in an ice cube tray ahead of time, you can use those cubes to create "instant pudding" and save yourself from having to wait while your mouth waters for your dessert to chill!

Servings: 2 | **Prep time:** 5 minutes + 30–60 minutes of soaking the dates | **Creation time:** 5–10 minutes (not including chill time)

1½ **tbsp (24 g) raw cacao or pure cocoa powder**

5 pitted dates, soaked 30–60 minutes

1 tsp vanilla

1 ripe avocado

Pinch of salt

2 tbsp (30 g) hazelnut butter, or sub nut butter of choice

Stevia to taste, optional

3–4 tbsp (45–60 ml) almond milk, or vegan milk of choice

2 almond milk ice cubes, optional, if you want instant mousse!

Combine all of the ingredients except almond milk and cubes in a high-speed blender. Add the almond milk and cubes a little at a time as you process until the mixture is the texture of mousse.

If you used almond milk ice cubes, you can enjoy immediately. If not, chill for 1 hour before serving.

WEEK 6

OVERVIEW

	MON	TUES	WED	THURS	FRI	SAT	SUN
BREAKFAST	Wonderful Watermelon Smoothie	Cinnamon Bun Smoothie	Lively Lemon Basil Smoothie	Ramp up Raspberry Cacao Smoothie	So Fresh & So Clean Smoothie	Carrot Cake Oatmeal	Polenta Pleaser and Fresh Cashew Milk
LUNCH	Jumpin' Black Bean & Avocado Salad	Luscious Leftovers	Quinoa Flat Tummy Tabouli Salad	Luscious Leftovers	Marry Me Mango-Avocado Spinach Salad	Luscious Leftovers	
SNACK	Fresh Fruit of Choice	Fresh Fruit of Choice	Fresh Fruit of Choice	Fresh Fruit of Choice	Fresh Fruit of Choice	Fresh Fruit of Choice	Fresh Fruit of Choice
DINNER	Magic Mushroom Millet Soup & Sautéed Sesame Cabbage	Mac Daddy & Cheese with Broccoli	Busta' Black Bean Soup with Avocado	Teasingly Truffled Yam Fries & Apple Raisin Coleslaw	Queen B Quinoa Soup & Sweet Potato Coconut Mash	Tempt Me Thai Tofu-Mushroom Endive Wraps	Baller Baked Cauliflower Mash with Sweet Peas & Steamed Summer Squash
TREAT	X	X	Give Me Abs Apple Surprise	X	X	X	Fresh Double Mint Pudding
WORKOUT	Cross-Train (full body focus)	Cardio + Yoga	Cross-Train (upper body focus)	Cardio	Cross-Train (lower body focus)	Yoga + Cardio	Off/Rest

GROCERY LIST - WEEK 6

LIQUIDS

- Vegan milk of choice (46 oz [1.4 L])
- Coconut water (8 oz [235 ml])
- Vegetable broth (58 oz [1.7 L])

FRUIT

- Apple (1)
- Avocados (2)
- Bananas (4)
- Lemons (3)
- Lime (½) (or sub lime juice)
- Mango (1)
- Pears (2)
- Watermelon cubes (2½ cups [225 g])
- Frozen raspberries (1 cup [250 g])
- Dates (13)
- Raisins (¾ cup [110 g])

LEAFY GREENS

- Baby spinach (7 handfuls)
- Dandelion greens or sub spinach (1 handful)
- Salad greens of choice (1 handful)

VEGETABLES

- Bell pepper, red (1)
- Carrots (3)
- Cabbage, green (1 head)
- Cauliflower (1 small head)
- Celery (1 bunch)
- Cucumber (1)
- Grape tomatoes (½ cup [75 g])
- Jalapeño (optional) (½–1)
- Mushrooms, cremini (1½ 8 oz [225 g] packages)
- Mushrooms, (two 8 oz [225 g] packages)
- Onion, green (6 stalks)
- Onion, red (1–1 ½)
- Summer squash (1)
- Tomato (1½)
- Yams or sweet potatoes (4 small)
- Frozen broccoli florets (2 cups [150 g])
- Frozen sweet green peas (1½ cups [195 g])
- Diced tomatoes (one 15-oz [425-g] can)
- Tomato paste (one 6-oz [170-g] can)

PREP DAY

- Cook quinoa
- Chop vegetables for salads and soups
- Steam broccoli
- Steam cauliflower
- Cook sweet potatoes
- Press tofu

SUPER FOOD SMOOTHIE RECIPES

We will be recycling the smoothies from week three this week. Feel free to have some fun playing around with the ingredients, putting your own spin on the smoothies. You now have five weeks of experience to help you be creative with the recipes while keeping them healthy and in line with the Six Weeks to Sexy Abs Plan!

CARROT CAKE Oatmeal

Cake? For breakfast? On a diet? You'd better believe it! If you enjoy carrot cake as much as I do, you will be pleased with this recipe. This sweet, nutty meal will boost your day with great energy release and a metabolic system charge up, leaving you feeling content and ready for anything. Quick to prepare and containing a cardiovascular boost from the carrots, it's a great inclusion to the menu.

Servings: 1 large portion | **Prep time:** 5 minutes | **Creation time:** 15 minutes

½ cup (40 g) rolled oats

¾ cup (175 ml) water

½ cup (120 ml) nut milk

¼ cup (25 g) shredded carrots

3–4 tbsp (27–36 g) raisins

¼ tsp cinnamon

⅛ tsp nutmeg

3–4 tbsp (24–32 g) walnut pieces

Stevia to taste

OPTIONAL TOPPERS

Coconut shreds

Splash of vegan creamer

Bring the oats, water, milk, carrots, raisins, cinnamon and nutmeg to boiling and reduce heat.

Simmer for about 7 to 10 minutes, stirring occasionally, until the oatmeal becomes thick.

Stir in the walnut pieces and add stevia to reach the desired sweetness.

Top with the optional coconut shreds and creamer. Enjoy!

POLENTA PLEASER AND FRESH CASHEW *Milk*

Spinach and mushroom is a classic mix, and when rounded off with the rich crunch of pine nuts and melted vegan cheese over polenta, this dish will stimulate and satisfy your taste buds! With high levels of Vitamin E, K and A, you can be sure you're feeding your body what it needs to be healthy and drop those extra pounds. Plus it's easy to make!

POLENTA PLEASER

Servings: 2 meal-size portions | **Prep time:** 5-10 minutes | **Creation time:** 15-20 minutes

1 package of pre-cooked, packaged polenta

1-2 tsp (5-10 g) refined coconut oil

1 tsp extra virgin olive oil

1 garlic clove, minced

2 cups (140 g) sliced mushrooms

3 large handfuls spinach

¼ cup (30 g) Daiya mozzarella shreds, optional, plus more for serving

2 tbsp (18 g) pine nuts, optional

Sea salt and pepper to taste

Slice the polenta into ¼–½-inch (6.35–12.7 mm) pieces.

Heat a large skillet with 1 teaspoon coconut oil to medium-high. Add as many polenta slices as will fit in the pan in a single layer.

Also, heat a large sauté pan with 1 teaspoon olive oil to medium. Add the garlic and mushrooms and sauté until the mushrooms become tender, about 5 minutes. Then add the spinach and continue to sauté until the spinach has wilted, another 2 to 3 minutes.

Once the polenta slices have browned on one side, about 5 to 7 minutes, flip them, and sprinkle the Daiya shreds on top, if you're using them. Cook until the second side browns.

Place the polenta slices on a plate. Add the spinach and mushroom mixture over the polenta. Sprinkle the pine nuts, salt and pepper to taste, and optional additional Daiya shreds on top.

FRESH CASHEW MILK

Servings: 2 | **Prep time:** 5 minutes + 6 hours of soaking the cashews | **Creation time:** 5-10 minutes

1 cup (145 g) raw cashews, soaked 6-8 hours

4 cups (945 ml) water

3-4 Medjool dates, pitted

1 tsp vanilla extract

Pinch of sea salt

¼ tsp cinnamon, optional

Place all of the ingredients in a high-speed blender.

Process, working your way up to the highest speed, until fully blended. If your blender is not able to fully blend the cashews with the water, you may need to strain the mixture through a nut milk bag.

That's it!

JUMPIN' BLACK BEAN & AVOCADO *Salad*

I describe this dish as simple, clean and delightful with powerful health benefits. The healthy oleic acid from avocado helps your body to use stored fat as fuel, and legumes have been shown to reduce the risks of cardiovascular disease and type 2 diabetes. The high levels of fiber in this salad will also aid your digestion and promote a healthy metabolism, supporting your goals of a sexy, lean body.

Servings: 2 | **Prep time:** 5-10 minutes | **Creation time:** 5 minutes

1 (15 oz [425 g]) can black beans, drained and rinsed

½ cup (75 g) diced red bell pepper

½ cup (75 g) halved grape tomatoes

1 green onion, diced

1 tbsp (1 g) chopped cilantro

½ a jalapeño, diced, optional

1 tbsp (15 ml) extra virgin olive oil

1 tbsp (15 ml) fresh lime juice

Sea salt to taste

Black pepper to taste

1 avocado, sliced

Combine the black beans, red bell pepper, tomatoes, green onion, cilantro and optional jalapeño in a large bowl.

Toss in the olive oil, lime juice, salt and pepper.

Last, carefully fold in the avocado slices so that they do not become mushy and serve.

QUINOA FLAT TUMMY TABOULI *Salad*

This variation of traditional tabouli will have your taste buds popping in minutes! Traditional bulgur wheat is replaced with quinoa for added protein and nutrients. Use cucumber for a more savory salad, or apple for a salad with added sweet tones. The red onion also helps keep blood sugars low and promotes weight loss.

Servings: 1 meal-size portion | **Prep time:** 15 minutes | **Creation time:** 5 minutes

1 tbsp (15 ml) extra virgin olive oil

1 tbsp (15 ml) lime juice, or sub lemon juice

¼ tsp sea salt to taste

Black pepper to taste

1 cup (185 g) quinoa, cooked

1 cup (180 g) diced tomato

1 cup (120 g) diced cucumber or 1 cup (150 g) diced Granny Smith apple

½ cup (80 g) diced red onion

½ cup (75 g) diced red bell pepper or bell pepper of choice

½ cup (30 g) fresh Italian parsley, chopped

¼ cup (24 g) fresh mint leaves, chopped, optional

Salad greens, optional

In a large bowl whisk together the olive oil, lime juice, salt and pepper.

Add the quinoa, vegetables and herbs and toss.

Eat on its own or place on some salad greens.

MARRY ME MANGO-AVOCADO SPINACH *Salad*

Rich, creamy avocado paired with sweet succulent mango and rounded off with an aromatic curry dressing, this is a truly tasty salad. This recipe has you taking in good fats, antioxidants and the vitamins and minerals you need, in addition to some glorious flavors. Eat slowly and savor every bite!

Servings: 1 meal-size salad and 2 portions of dressing | **Prep time:** 10 minutes | **Creation time:** 10 minutes if you make the dressing, 5 minutes if you use store-bought

2 handfuls of baby spinach

1 small mango, peeled and sliced

1 small avocado, sliced

¼ cup (15 g) parsley leaves, chopped

2 tbsp (18 g) sunflower seeds

DRESSING (OR USE SIMILAR STORE-BOUGHT VERSION)

2 tbsp (30 ml) extra virgin olive oil

2 tbsp (30 ml) fresh orange juice

2 tbsp (30 ml) water

3 pitted dates, soaked, or ½ tbsp (7 ml) pure maple syrup

⅛ tsp curry powder

⅛ tsp sea salt

Combine the spinach, mango, avocado and parsley in a large bowl.

In a small bowl, combine the dressing ingredients. Use a fork to mush the dates and then whisk everything together, or use a blender or food processor to combine all of the ingredients.

Pour the dressing over the salad and add the sunflower seeds on top.

MAGIC MUSHROOM MILLET *Soup* & SAUTÉED SESAME CABBAGE

In this slow-cooker soup recipe we use the grain-like seed millet, which boasts a high nutrient content and supports heart health. It's also used by many cultures around the globe as an alternative to wheat. The sautéed sesame cabbage, as well as looking and tasting delicious, will also support healthy digestion.

MAGIC MUSHROOM MILLET SOUP

Servings: 2-3 meal-size portions | **Prep time:** 10-15 minutes | **Creation time:** 5 minutes kitchen time + 8 hours cooking in the slow cooker

½ cup (85 g) millet	Combine all of the ingredients in your slow cooker and cook for 8 hours on the low setting.
5 cups (1.2 L) vegetable broth or bouillon	
1 (8 oz [225 g]) package sliced button mushrooms	
½ a red onion, diced	
3 garlic cloves, minced	
1 stalk celery, diced	
¼ cup (15 g) fresh parsley, chopped	
2 tbsp (30 ml) vegan Worcester sauce	
2 tbsp (30 ml) Bragg Liquid Aminos	
1 tbsp (15 ml) extra virgin olive oil, optional	
⅛ tsp black pepper to taste	

SAUTÉED SESAME CABBAGE

Servings: 2 side portions | **Prep time:** 5-8 minutes | **Creation time:** 10 minutes

1 tsp sesame oil	Heat a sauté pan with the sesame oil to medium-high heat. Place the garlic in the pan and sauté for 30 seconds and then add the cabbage, salt and pepper. Sauté until tender, about 6 to 8 minutes.
2 cloves garlic, minced	
4 cups (360 g) chopped green cabbage	Stir in the sesame seeds and serve.
Sea salt and pepper to taste	
1 tbsp (8 g) sesame seeds	

BUSTA' BLACK BEAN *Soup* WITH AVOCADO

This highly filling soup is full of fiber and healthy fats with a surprising freshness from the celery and cilantro combination. Long hailed the savior of weight loss dieters, avocado is packed full of monounsaturated oleic acid for a slow release of energy that will keep you perky for hours! You have the option to enhance the flavors with a kick of jalapeño.

Servings: 4 dinner-size portions | **Prep time:** 10–15 minutes | **Creation time:** 30–40 minutes using stovetop, or 8 hours in the slow cooker + 5 minutes kitchen time

½ an onion, diced

2 cloves garlic (or 1 tbsp [10 g] of chopped bottled garlic)

½ a green or red bell pepper, diced

1 large celery rib with leaves attached, diced

½ a jalapeño pepper, diced, optional

2 tbsp (30 ml) extra virgin olive oil

4 cups (945 ml) vegetable broth

3 cups (515 g) black beans

1 large vine-ripe tomato, chopped

1 tbsp (2.5 g) chopped fresh basil, or sub 1 tsp dried

½ tsp dried oregano

2 bay leaves

⅓ cup (5 g) chopped fresh cilantro, or sub 1½ tbsp (3 g) dried cilantro

1–2 tbsp (12–24 g) nutritional yeast, optional

¼ tsp sea salt

Black pepper to taste

½ a small avocado, sliced

STOVETOP

Sauté the onion, garlic, peppers, celery and optional jalapeño in a big pot with olive oil over medium heat until the vegetables are tender, about 8 to 10 minutes, stirring regularly.

Now add the vegetable broth and stir. Turn the heat up to medium-high, and when the water boils, add the black beans, tomatoes, basil, oregano, bay leaves and cilantro.

When it boils again, turn it down to simmer and cook for around 15 minutes.

Adding nutritional yeast into the soup during the last few minutes of cooking smoothes the flavor and adds nutrients.

Leave the soup chunky or use an immersion blender for a smooth and creamy style soup.

Before serving, add salt and pepper and garnish with a few cilantro leaves.

Serve the sliced avocado on the side with a pinch of sea salt and black pepper, or place the avocado on top of the soup to eat.

SLOW COOKER

Combine all of the ingredients except the nutritional yeast, avocado, salt and pepper, in a slow cooker. Cook for about 7 to 8 hours on low.

Add the optional nutritional yeast during the last 30 minutes of cooking.

Leave chunky or use an immersion blender for a smooth and creamy style soup.

Before serving, add salt and pepper and garnish with a few cilantro leaves.

Serve the sliced avocado on the side with a pinch of sea salt and black pepper, or place the avocado on top of the soup to eat.

QUEEN B QUINOA *Soup* & SWEET POTATO COCONUT *Mash*

Quinoa and cannellini beans are royalty when it comes to leading nutrition! This soup has it all, including big flavor and heartiness. There's not even too much chopping for this one. You'll be able to throw everything in the slow cooker quickly, and next time you look you will be psyched at the meal you'll find waiting for you! With this lavish sweet potato mash on the side—one of my absolute favorites—you will be totally satisfied.

QUEEN B QUINOA SOUP

Servings: 2-3 meal-size portions | **Prep time:** 10 minutes | **Creation time:** 8-10 hours in slow cooker on low or 3½ on high

1 (15 oz [425 g]) can canellini beans, no salt added, undrained	Combine all of the ingredients in the slow cooker and heat on high around 3½ hours or low around 8 hours.
½ cup (85 g) quinoa (raw)	
3 cups (710 ml) vegetable broth	
1 cup (130 g) chopped carrots	
1 can (15 oz [425 g]) diced tomatoes	
1 can (6 oz [170 g]) tomato paste	
2 stalks green onion, diced	
2 cups (140 g) sliced cremini mushrooms	
2 cloves garlic, minced	
1 tbsp (4 g) chopped fresh oregano	
1½ tbsp (3.75 g) chopped fresh basil	
1 tsp chili powder	
¼ tsp sea salt to taste	
Black pepper to taste	
Cayenne pepper and/or hot sauce to taste, optional	

SWEET POTATO COCONUT MASH

Servings: 1-2 | **Prep time:** 2 minutes (not including cooking the sweet potatoes) | **Creation time:** 5 minutes

2 medium-size sweet potatoes, cooked*	Combine all of the ingredients in your high-speed blender and process until smooth and creamy.
1 tbsp (15 ml) culinary coconut milk or 1½ tbsp (924 ml) full fat coconut milk	
¼ tsp cinnamon to taste	*See page 117 for sweet potato cooking instructions.
Dash of sea salt to taste	

Mac DADDY & CHEESE WITH BROCCOLI

A take on the American classic, this mac and cheese recipe gives you a huge helping of plant-protein from the pasta, and vitamins C, B, K and A, as well as iron and zinc from the broccoli—no wonder I consider it a super meal!

Servings: 2 | **Prep time:** 2 minutes | **Creation time:** 10-15 minutes

2 cups (310 g) frozen broccoli florets, or sub fresh

½ a package Explore Asia Edamame & Mung Bean Fettuccini

¼ cup (60 ml) plain-flavored almond or flax milk

¾ cup (100 g) Daiya mozzarella shreds to taste

Sea salt and pepper to taste

Steam the frozen broccoli according to the instructions on the package.

Bring a large pot of water to boil. Add the pasta, bring back to boiling, reduce heat and cook at a rolling boil, about 5 to 7 minutes, until al dente.

Drain and rinse the pasta using a colander.

Place the pot back on the burner set to medium/medium-low and add the milk and Daiya mozzarella shreds.

Stir until the cheese melts and forms a sauce with the milk. Add the broccoli florets and pasta and combine thoroughly. Add sea salt and pepper to taste.

TEASINGLY TRUFFLED YAM *Fries* & APPLE RAISIN *Coleslaw*

Love fries? Here you go—delicious, guilt-free fries with flare. Yams can help along your digestion and speed up your metabolism. They're also a great source of B-complex vitamins, which help to regulate your body's metabolic functions and are also a good source of important minerals. Try them out in this easy to prepare recipe.

This coleslaw is so fantastic and with the combo of cabbage, apples and raisins, it's almost like dinner and dessert in one!

TEASINGLY TRUFFLED YAM FRIES

Servings: 3 | **Prep time:** 10 minutes | **Creation time:** 10 minutes in the kitchen + 30 minutes in the oven

4 small yams **2 tbsp (30 g) coconut oil, melted, plus more for greasing** **1 tsp truffle sea salt, or sub sea salt**	Preheat oven to 400°F (200°C). Peel the yams and cut into even-size French fry–shaped pieces. Toss the yam slices with the coconut oil and truffle salt—you can use regular sea salt or other seasoning salt if you don't have truffle. Grease a dark pan with coconut oil and place the yam slices evenly in a single layer on the pan without overlapping. Cook for about 30 minutes total, until slightly browned, flipping them halfway through at around 15 minutes.

APPLE RAISIN COLESLAW

Servings: 3-4 | **Prep time:** 15 minutes | **Creation time:** 10 minutes

5 cups (350 g) shredded green and/or red cabbage **½ a red bell pepper, diced** **1 green onion, diced** **¼ cup (35 g) raisins** **¼ cup (60 g) vegan mayo** **¼ tsp salt** **⅛ cup (8 g) loosely packed fresh dill, chopped** **¼–½ large lemon, juiced** **2 tbsp (30 ml) apple cider vinegar** **Black pepper to taste**	Combine cabbage, bell pepper, onion and raisins in a large bowl. In a small bowl, combine the mayo, salt, dill, lemon juice, apple cider vinegar and black pepper, and whisk together. Add to the cabbage mixture and toss thoroughly.

TEMPT ME THAI TOFU-MUSHROOM ENDIVE *Wraps*

Once they're all wrapped up, these look especially inviting on your plate. The sauce packs a lot of flavor; the tofu soaks up that delicious flavor and provides complete protein. Plus you'll get all the nutrients from the mushrooms and endives—which are especially high in vitamin K, giving your blood a helping hand in keeping your system clear and running right. The water chestnuts give an important crunch to vary the texture and leave you satisfied.

Servings: 2–3 meal-size portions | **Prep time:** 10–15 minutes (not including pressing the tofu) | **Creation time:** 20 minutes

SAUCE (OR USE A STORE-BOUGHT VEGAN THAI PEANUT SAUCE)

4 tbsp (60 g) natural peanut butter, or sub almond butter

2 tbsp (30 ml) Bragg Liquid Aminos (or Tamari)

1 garlic clove, pressed (or ⅛ tsp garlic powder)

2–4 tsp (10–20 ml) hot sauce (depending on how spicy you like it)

2 tsp (5 g) fresh grated ginger (or ½ tsp ground ginger)

2 tbsp (30 ml) apple cider vinegar

2–4 tbsp (30–60 ml) vegetable broth (unsalted)

Black pepper to taste

1 head of endive

½–1 tbsp (7–15 g) refined coconut oil, or sub sesame oil

1 (1 lb [455 g]) block extra-firm tofu, pressed* and cut into the smallest cubes possible

1 (8 oz [225 g]) package cremini mushrooms (aka baby bellas), diced

2 green onions, diced

1 cup (235 ml) water chestnuts, diced into tiny pieces

Whisk together the sauce ingredients in a small bowl and set aside.

Slice off the hard bottom part of the endive and then gently separate the leaves. You will probably need to make a new slice every couple leaves. You will only use the outside leaves that are large enough to use as wraps, so save the inside portion in the fridge for use in a salad. Set aside.

Heat the coconut oil in a sauté pan to medium heat.

Add the tofu and sauté until it begins to brown, about 10 to 12 minutes. You may be able to turn the heat to medium-high to speed the process, as long as the tofu is not sticking to the pan.

Add the mushrooms, onion and water chestnuts and continue to sauté until the mushrooms begin to become tender, another 5 to 7 minutes.

Add the sauce and continue to mix and sauté for another 2 to 3 minutes.

*See page 43 for instructions on pressing tofu.

BALLER BAKED CAULIFLOWER *Mash*
WITH SWEET PEAS & STEAMED SUMMER SQUASH

Easy to prepare and to eat, this dish keeps your kitchen time and work level low. Its non-starchy nature means cauliflower is a perfect part of the meal plan, as it will help you lose weight quickly, especially when you're using it to replace white potatoes!

BALLER BAKED CAULIFLOWER MASH WITH SWEET PEAS

Servings: 3 | **Prep time:** 5-10 minutes | **Creation time:** 30-40 minutes

1 small head of cauliflower

4 cloves garlic, whole

1½ cups (195 g) frozen sweet green peas

2-3 tbsp (30-45 g) vegan buttery spread, or sub extra virgin olive oil

¼ tsp sea salt to taste

Back pepper to taste

¼ cup (15 g) fresh parsley, chopped, or sub 2 tsp (1 g) dried parsley

¼ cup (10 g) basil leaves, chopped, or sub 2 tsp (1 g) dried basil

Remove the leaves and hard bottom from the cauliflower.

Cut into pieces so that it will fit in the steamer—the smaller the pieces, the quicker they will cook.

Steam the cauliflower and whole garlic cloves until tender, about 10 to 15 minutes.

To cook the peas, bring a pot of water to boil. Add frozen peas and bring back to boil. Reduce heat and cook at a rolling boil for 5 to 7 minutes until fork tender. Drain.

Preheat the oven to broil.

Combine the cauliflower and garlic with the buttery spread, salt and pepper in your high-speed blender and process until smooth. Alternatively, you can place all of the ingredients in a pot or bowl and use an immersion blender to process.

Stir in the sweet green peas, parsley and basil.

Pour or scoop the mash into a glass pan and broil until it's browned on top, about 6 to 8 minutes.

STEAMED SUMMER SQUASH

Servings: 2 sides | **Prep time:** 2 minutes | **Creation time:** 15 minutes

1 summer squash, or sub zucchini, cut lengthwise

½ tbsp (7 ml) extra virgin olive oil or vegan buttery spread

Sea salt to taste

Black pepper to taste

Steam squash halves using a steamer basket in a pot on the stove until they are fork tender, about 8 to 10 minutes.

Place squash halves on a plate, open side facing up.

Score the squash with a fork and then drizzle with olive oil, or buttery spread, and salt and pepper to taste.

FRESH DOUBLE MINT *Pudding*

These frozen treats are filled with all around goodness! From the potassium-filled banana and protein-packed tofu to the heart healthy fats of the avocado, sweetness of the dates and the richness of the pure vanilla. The mint leaves add an extra level of fresh mint taste, as well as aiding digestion and improving respiration. Healthy and delicious!

Servings: 4 | **Prep time:** 5 minutes | **Creation time:** 5–10 minutes

1 frozen banana

1 avocado

¼ **package silken tofu**

3–4 **sprigs mint leaves**

1 tsp vanilla

3 dates, pitted

Stevia powder to taste

2 tbsp (30 g) vegan chocolate chips (raw cacao or unsweetened/semi-sweet chocolate chips)

Process all of the ingredients except the chocolate chips in a high-speed blender and blend until smooth and creamy.

Fold in the chocolate chips.

Chill for 15 minutes in the freezer and enjoy.

GIVE ME ABS APPLE *Surprise*

Apple and cinnamon is a combination that people have been enjoying for ages. This recipe uses this great combo to create one of the most simple and delectable treats you've ever made.

Servings: 2 | **Prep time:** 5 minutes | **Creation time:** 5–10 minutes

1 apple, cored and sliced in ¼–½"
(6–12 mm) slices lengthwise

4 tbsp (60 g) almond butter, or sub
nut butter of choice

3–4 tbsp (27–36 g) raisins or diced
dates

Cinnamon to taste

Stevia to taste, optional

3 tbsp (45 g) unsweetened coconut
flakes to taste

Place the apple slices on a plate in a single layer. Spread the nut butter on the apple slices. Place the raisins or diced dates on top of the nut butter. Sprinkle cinnamon and optional stevia sweetener to taste, and garnish with the coconut flakes.

CHAPTER III

MAINTAINING YOUR
Sexy FIT ABS

Eating the Sexy Fit Vegan Way Ongoing

After completing the Six Weeks to Sexy Abs Plan, you are likely feeling better than you have in years, maybe decades! So now what? It's time to discuss what it's going to take to maintain the sexy abs you've earned. It's possible that in addition to loving how you look and feel, and enjoying the new foods and different meals you've experienced, you may be ready to change things up. Maybe the smoothie in the morning works perfectly for you and you want to continue with it during the week. Or maybe you find that you want something warm to eat in the mornings so oatmeal works better for you, and a smoothie makes the perfect lunch or snack. It's time to experiment, switch things up and discover the routine that works best for you!

The basic guidelines for a Sexy Fit Vegan® lifestyle are similar to those for the Six Weeks to Sexy Abs Plan, we simply give you more freedom to change the structure, and allow room for you to find a balance between ideal, whole plant foods and less-than-ideal "treats"—we'll get to "treats" in a minute. It's all about finding the balance that gives you joy and satisfaction while allowing you to feel your best physically and maintain the toned midsection you've earned!

Eating the Sexy Fit Vegan® way is a matter of reducing, replacing and recycling. Let me explain.

Reduce, Replace, Recycle

Reduce and/or eliminate animal products and other unhealthy foods from your diet. You're on a roll after completing the Six Weeks to Sexy Abs Plan, so keep the momentum going! You've made it through the toughest part. You've survived the withdrawals of unhealthy and addictive foods, you've successfully broken the chain of bad habits and you're thriving. Now keep moving, full-steam ahead, because it only gets easier from here on out!

Replace animal products and unhealthy foods with healthier, plant-based foods. Sounds simple enough, right? It actually is! Today, we have so many alternatives to animal products readily available, it's just a matter of finding the ones that are both good for your body and your taste buds. Instead of ice cream, try out So Delicious Coconut Milk Frozen Dessert for example. Replace greasy potato chips with baked lentil chips. Double up on the beans or use Beyond Meat instead of meat in your burrito. Replace inorganic with organic foods whenever the option is available. Whether you are preparing food at home or are out to eat, you now have tools to make healthful decisions that will serve you better.

Recycle healthy recipes that you discover and love. Incorporate simple variations in your favorite recipes to add variety and prevent boredom. No need to reinvent the wheel every day. The Six Weeks to Sexy Abs menu gave you a great place to start with a set of base recipes. Now pick the meals you enjoyed and experiment with ways to mix things up. For example, if you really enjoy the Spaghetti Squash Marinara (page 59), think of the spaghetti squash as your base and "recycle" it by dressing it up with garlic and olive oil or Cauliflower Alfredo Sauce (page 86). All of a sudden, you've made a meal with a completely different feel without much added thought or effort. Zucchini spirals, cauliflower mash, stir-fry and mung bean pasta are more great examples of healthy bases that can easily turn into new dishes with a simple change of herbs, spices and sauces.

Although the Sexy Fit Vegan® way of eating is primarily composed of whole plant foods, unlike the intense Six Weeks to Sexy Abs Meal Plan, there is more wiggle room for the inclusion of less-than-ideal foods. Craving spaghetti and meatballs and low on time or energy? Grab some frozen, premade vegan meatballs to add to mung bean pasta, spaghetti squash or whole grain pasta on occasion. Find yourself missing filet of fish? Gardein brand makes an amazing vegan fish filet you can treat yourself to. I say go for it if that's what you need to stick with a plant-based diet! It's simply important to be aware that these foods are processed and therefore considered "treats." We don't want to habitually make them part of our daily routine.

I'll give you a personal example. During football season, my Sunday Funday involves drinking some beer and eating vegan wings while I watch a game or two. Yes, empty calories and processed food! It's part of the balance my lifestyle holds. It's an opportunity for me to relax and splurge while still staying true to a plant-based diet, share in a social activity I enjoy with friends and introduce others to vegan substitutes for foods they may otherwise think they can't give up. It's a great feeling when an avid wing-eater tries my Gardein wings and loves them so much he orders them for himself—and not just once, but every Sunday from there on out!

Now it's your turn. Explore the balance that works for you. Everyone's body runs differently and it will take some experimentation for you to figure out the perfect plan for you. The great part about it is that you now have the knowledge and experience of the Six Weeks to Sexy Abs Plan to fall back on. If you ever find yourself creeping back into old bad habits, or your jeans start to feel too tight around your waist, get back on the plan for a while. It's healthy and delicious and it's sure to quickly get you back on track!

Strong is Sexy: Exercise as a Way of Life

The Sexy Fit Vegan® lifestyle includes finding effective forms of exercise that you actually enjoy. Enjoyment is a key to consistency, and consistency is essential for success. If you dread every workout, you're going to be miserable and that's the opposite of what we're going for! Which types of workouts give you an "exercise high"? If you happened to get addicted, would that be such a terrible thing? Not with exercise as your drug! For me, muay thai is my "drug" of choice. It's certainly not the only activity I do as part of my routine, however. Variety is also important to keep our bodies balanced and prevent boredom. A routine that consists of a combination of cross-training, cardio and stretching is a great formula for a strong, lean body and healthy heart.

Seek support! It's always helpful to have others to hold you accountable for what you say you're going to do. Find a workout partner and schedule training sessions together, or commit to meeting a friend for kickboxing class every Wednesday, and another to take spinning with you every Friday. This can make all the difference in the world, not only to help you stick to a routine, but also to make your routine fun! To top it off, including others in your plans and sharing your progress gives you the opportunity to give back and be a positive influence on the people you care about!

Let's touch on sleep. We often put a heavy emphasis on the importance of exercise and fail to acknowledge the value of sleep. With exercise comes trauma to our bodies. During weight training, we actually cause micro tears in our muscle fibers. Optimal rest combined with proper nutrition is what allows our muscles to repair, rebuild and strengthen. During sleep is when much of this recovery occurs. Additionally, adequate sleep helps us maintain our memory and learning abilities, boosts mood, plays a role in a healthy metabolism and keeps our immune systems strong. Splurge on a quality mattress, take a warm bath before bed, wear earplugs if you have a snoring partner—whatever you need to do to get a good night's sleep. Becoming your strongest, sexiest you depends on it!

CHAPTER IV

TOOLS & TIPS TO MAKE YOUR LIFE *Easier*

Staying Stocked with Staples

Time to create your very own list of staples to stock your fridge so you'll be ready to eat the Sexy Fit Vegan® way ongoing! Use the staple ingredients we used throughout the Six Weeks to Sexy Abs as a starting point. Then simply add or subtract items based on your likes and dislikes. You probably discovered some new foods you didn't even know you liked that you can now make a part of your regular eating routine! The one addition I recommend adding to the list and your nutrition regiment is vitamin B12. It is the one nutrient that we no longer get eating plants. Simply speaking, B12 is found in soil, and the sanitation process produce goes through before it hits the market removes all traces of this important vitamin. It is luckily an incredibly cheap and easy vitamin to add to our daily dietary routine.

Based on what you've learned and experienced, it's your job to fine-tune your diet to make it one that you love and that makes you feel your best from the inside out. The most important reason to always keep your kitchen stocked with these staples is so that you can easily put together a healthy snack or meal to satisfy a hungry tummy, even when you feel "starving" and are in a hurry. You know what I'm talking about? We all get there! Once we get to that advanced stage of hunger, our brains often don't function well enough to make the best decisions. We therefore must set ourselves up to have only positive choices available. That way, whatever decision we make will be a good one!

Smart Grocery Shopping

Food shopping seems like it would be second nature after doing it our entire adult lives. If you have the habit of rushing through the aisles, grabbing products labeled "Healthy" and "All Natural," it's time to break the mold and learn to shop smart.

Shopping smart first and foremost involves reading nutrition labels. Start with the ingredients. What are the first three ingredients? If there is something that you know is unhealthy, or you can't even pronounce one of the ingredients, put that box right back on the shelf. If the list of ingredients is long, that's also a bad sign. If you find the ingredients healthy enough, move on to the nutrition facts. Look at the serving size first so you know the amount of food the facts apply to. For example, you may see 6 grams of sugar on the label for granola thinking that goes for a cup—because that's how much you think you would eat for breakfast—when the servings size is actually a quarter of a cup. Now all of a sudden the cup of granola you plan to eat has 24 grams of sugar. That's quite a difference. You then must take into consideration where the sugar is coming from. Does the granola contain raisins and no refined sugar? Then ok, it's coming from a whole food! If the sugar is refined however, it's time to think twice. This same philosophy goes for the fat content—stay far away from any product containing trans fats—and carbohydrates. Just remember that whole, plant food ingredients are always best and you will be able to make informed decisions at the store.

Shopping smart also means staying away from the grocery store when you're hungry or in a hurry. Like a sex addict in an adult toy store, you'll be powerless to resist temptation and will undoubtedly walk out with products you don't need! Plan ahead. Schedule your trip to the grocery store when you have a satisfied stomach and enough time to read labels and make informed decisions.

Substitutions/Conversions

The recipes in the Six Weeks to Sexy Abs Meal Plan contain many options to make it easy to customize based on your time restrictions and ingredients you are more likely to have/not have available to use. Here are some of the most common substitutions you may want or need to make.

Herbs

The general rule when it comes to fresh vs. dried herbs is 1 tablespoon (~6 g) chopped fresh herb = 1 teaspoon dried herb. Fresh herbs are usually the tastiest way to go, but they're also the more expensive and less practical way to go. Depending on what you have stocked in your kitchen and what you're willing to spend at the store, the decision is up to you.

Garlic

The general rule for fresh garlic vs. minced garlic in a jar vs. garlic powder: Fresh garlic and minced garlic in a jar are very different than garlic powder. It's one of the more important ingredients to stick with fresh or jarred when called for in the recipes. Fortunately, fresh garlic has the benefit of staying good for quite a while in the fridge so it's easy to stock. Minced garlic in a jar has the advantage of saving you from chopping. Your call! Here are the substitution rules: 1 clove of garlic = 1 teaspoon chopped garlic = ½ teaspoon minced garlic = ⅛ teaspoon garlic powder.

Vegetable Broth

Go with a low-sodium or sodium-free broth. This way you have more control over the type and amount of sodium in your meal. Substituting vegetable bouillon can be a money-saver and is an acceptable alternative.

Vegan Milk

There are many different types of nut, seed and grain-based milks on the market today. For the most part, the recipes call for the "vegan milk of your choice." Your job is to experiment and discover the types that you enjoy most. Whatever type you choose, select the unsweetened, plain flavor, unless otherwise noted. This way you can control the amount and type of sweetener you add. Often times we don't want the milk to be sweet at all, and when we do, we want to stay away from the processed sugars some of these products contain. Also, for savory dishes, the plain flavor is important to use as opposed to the vanilla option.

Extra Virgin Olive Oil vs. Vegan Buttery Spread

Several recipes give you an option between extra virgin olive oil (EVOO) and vegan buttery spread. Olive oil is the cleaner and healthier option. Why then do I even give the choice? Olive oil doesn't have that same buttery flavor that can be incredibly enjoyable in some dishes! Sometimes, even during the six weeks of the plan, you may need a little boost of familiar flavors you may be craving, and depriving yourself could take you down the rabbit hole! Read the nutrition label and ingredients before buying a tub of vegan butter though. Make sure it contains zero trans fats and zero hydrogenated or partially hydrogenated oils.

Cooking Oils

Did you know that using extra virgin olive oil and unrefined coconut oil for high heat cooking is toxic? It's a fact many people are unaware of—that these oils have a lower smoke point, or point at which they begin to decompose and chemical changes occur, causing them to become carcinogenic. Therefore, we'll be using oils that have a higher smoke point such as refined coconut oil, grape seed oil, avocado oil and refined sesame oil in the recipes that call for sautéing at temperatures above "medium" heat.

Made From Scratch vs. Store-Bought Sauces

The recipes often give you the option to either make your own dressing or sauce, or to buy them premade at the store. I'm leaving it up to you. It comes down to your time, energy and budget. The made-from-scratch versions are beneficial because you know exactly what is going into it. You know the quality and amounts of each ingredient and there are no preservatives whatsoever. The made-from-scratch versions usually come out cheaper because most in these recipes are made with staple foods you will already have stocked in your kitchen. The downside is that they tack on a few minutes of time and a bit more effort to your recipe prep and creation times. Not much, but if you are already pressed, it may mean the difference between your feeling like you have the time and energy to prepare the dish and feeling like you don't.

Canned vs. Dried Beans

Canned or boxed beans are incredibly convenient and offer just about the same health benefits as dried—so unless specified as dried, the beans in the recipes are canned/boxed. When possible, buy cans that specify "BPA Free" or go with the boxed packages. You're certainly welcome to soak and cook your own beans as well if you choose.

Salt

The recipes call for sea salt. The recommended types of salts are Pink Himalayan or Celtic Sea salt that contain no additives or chemicals. These are naturally derived salts with trace elements and minerals that we need. These salts are still very high in sodium and too much sodium is harmful to us, so be wary and keep your intake low or moderate.

Peanuts and Gluten

Although the sample meal plan is not free of peanuts or gluten free, the majority of recipes in this the Six Weeks to Sexy Abs Meal Plan don't contain either. The recipes that do generally suggest a substitution to replace those ingredients.

TOP INGREDIENTS YOU MAY BE
Unfamiliar WITH

Acai: The acai berry is an antioxidant and fiber-rich fruit harvested from acai palm trees found in South America. Said to have a wide range of health benefits, acai berries are often used in smoothies and breakfast bowls. You can sometimes find the fruit in the freezer section to buy and use in smoothies.

Amla: Also known as Indian Gooseberry, amla is a fruit with particularly strong free radical–fighting abilities. Free radicals cause damage to our cells and can lead to cancer. Amla contains even more antioxidant agents than blueberries, helping to prevent and repair free radical damage. Adding just a teaspoon of amla powder to your smoothie can exponentially increase the amount of antioxidants you take in and is therefore a recommended addition to your daily smoothies.

Bragg Liquid Aminos: This is a product made from soybeans, described as a liquid protein concentrate. It has a flavor similar to soy sauce and tamari, and I use it instead of soy sauce/tamari because it has very little sodium, and no added salt. Even the soy sauce/tamari labeled as "low sodium" contains high amounts of sodium. Bragg Liquid Aminos is also gluten free.

Buckwheat: Classified as a grain-like seed, buckwheat groats are great as part of breakfast cereal and can be used as a replacement for rice and other grains when called for in recipes. Buckwheat is high in health-promoting phytonutrients and insoluble fiber and does not contain gluten.

Cacao Powder/Nibs: Raw cacao powder comes from the cacao bean and is a top source of antioxidants, magnesium and iron. Cacao nibs are to cacao powder as chocolate chips are to cocoa powder. Cacao nibs are generally minimally processed to retain the health benefits, and contain much less sugar than any chocolate chips.

Chia Seeds: Mild and nutty in flavor, chia seeds are a good source of omega 3 fatty acids, calcium, protein, fiber and antioxidants. Unlike flaxseeds, chia seeds can be absorbed by our bodies in its seed form. Chia seeds will soak up liquid and expand, making them useful to create a gel-type texture. This also means they can expand in your tummy, contributing to an increased feeling of fullness.

Dates/Date Paste: The fruit of the date palm, dates are oddly wrinkled and brown on the outside, but deliciously sweet, chewy and packed full of nutrition. They are great to use as a whole plant–food sweetener on almost any sweet treat. They are easily digested and eaten in moderation, they have a wide range of health-promoting effects. The Medjool variety is particularly large and especially great for use in raw food desserts. Date paste is great to have around to make it easier to combine with other ingredients when preparing food. Date paste is sold premade in a jar, or you can make it yourself by simply mashing dates. Don't forget to remove the pit!

Edamame: Another name for whole soybeans. Edamame is convenient to buy frozen and cook in boiling water for around 5 to 7 minutes. You can buy these legumes in the shell, which is great for eating as a side dish or appetizer, or out of the shell, which is best for using in salads and other dishes.

Farro: This is an ancient grain with more health-promoting properties than many other whole grains. It's a heart-healthy complex carbohydrate that regulates blood sugars, stimulates the immune system and contains more protein than brown rice. It's great for use in all types of dishes from soups and salads to hot breakfast cereal bowls. It is not gluten free but contains less gluten than other varieties of wheat. I find it particularly great to use in slow-cooker soup recipes, as it remains intact and adds great texture to the meal.

Flax Meal: Ground from flaxseed, flaxseed meal is the preferred form to consume because your body can digest it. We're not able to breakdown whole flaxseed, and if you've ever eaten it, you have probably witnessed proof! Grinding the flaxseed does not remove any of the benefits, as flaxseed is concentrated in omega 3 fatty acids, fiber, protein and lignans, which give it antioxidant power. When added to a smoothie or oatmeal, there's no notable change in your meal's flavor.

Grape Seed Oil: This oil is typically extracted from the seeds of grapes used to make wine. It has a very high smoke point, which makes it acceptable to use for high-heat cooking. The smoke point is the temperature at which the oil begins to break down and becomes carcinogenic (toxic). Grape seed oil has a neutral flavor and has antioxidant properties, omega fatty acids and vitamin E. The downside is that it's usually chemically processed, so choosing one with labeling that specifies how it's processed is a good idea.

Hemp Seeds: One of the most nutrient-dense seeds that exists, hemp seeds are packed with easily digestible protein, essential fatty acids, B vitamins, magnesium and a whole array of other vitamins, minerals and phytonutrients. They have a pleasant flavor and are a great addition to smoothies, salads, cereals and even desserts. Buy raw "hulled" hemp seeds that have the outer shell removed so they are ready to consume.

Herbamare Seasoning: An organic, seasoning salt blend that can take just about any savory dish from bland to delicious. I use it all the time!

Jicama: A large bulbous root with thin tan skin and a white inside, jicama has a crunch similar to an apple and a somewhat neutral flavor.

Maca: A plant that grows in the Andes Mountains in Peru, maca has been used for centuries for medicinal purposes. Today, it's known to increase energy levels and is used to help treat chronic fatigue and sexual dysfunction, improve athletic performance and even increase sexual desire. You can buy it in powder form and add it to your smoothies; it's a worthwhile investment!

Millet: A grain-like seed, millet is a good source of several important minerals as well as B vitamins. It's a heart-healthy whole food and can be used in place of rice or other grains to increase nutrient content and add variety to your diet.

Mung Beans: Mung beans are a small green legume that has been popular in China for thousands of years. Packing a hard nutrient punch, mung beans are high in protein, fiber, potassium, magnesium and B vitamins. They can be eaten raw, usually as sprouts, or cooked and are especially great in soups. The brand Explore Asian makes a pasta from a combination of mung beans and soy beans.

Nutritional Yeast: Usually found in the bulk sections of health food stores, nutritional yeast, aka "nooch," is a form of inactive yeast. It gets its name because in has a high nutritional value with tons of B vitamins, including B12, folic acid, zinc, selenium and protein. It's also low in fat and free of gluten. Its "cheesy" flavor makes it a popular addition to plant-based recipes. It's awesome sprinkled on popcorn, and is often used in soups and to make cheesy types of sauces.

Quinoa: Classified as a grain-like seed, quinoa is one of the few plant foods that contains all nine essential amino acids, making it a complete protein. It's known for its high level of overall nutritional value compared with other whole grains. Light and nutty, quinoa can be used in countless dishes, as well as on its own as a side.

Stevia Powder/Liquid: Extracted from the herbal plant *Stevia rebaudiana*, which grows in parts of Brazil and Paraguay, stevia powder and liquid is much sweeter than sugar but with virtually no calories. It does not raise blood sugar levels. The processing methods vary, some being healthier and safer than others. I find it best to use in drinks, cereals, smoothies and desserts, just be careful because a little bit goes a long way and it will turn food bitter if you overdo it.

Tahini: A paste made from ground sesame seeds, tahini is a popular part of Middle Eastern cuisine. It's an important ingredient in hummus, as well as many dressings and sauces. It's also a good source for manganese, copper and omega fatty acids.

Tamari: A type of soy sauce, tamari tastes like traditional soy sauce but is made without, or with very little, wheat. If you need to avoid gluten, make sure the bottle is specifically labeled "gluten free." It's very high in sodium, so it's also a good idea to buy the "lower sodium" version, being aware that it still contains a high level. To reduce sodium intake, use Bragg Liquid Aminos as most of my recipes suggest.

Tempeh: A fermented soybean product, tempeh is minimally processed, super healthy and packed with protein. It's packaged as a patty for you to slice, or as precut slices. Some tempeh on the market has additional grains and seeds added. Some tempeh is also pre-seasoned and/or pre-cooked. It makes a particularly good bacon substitute.

Textured Vegetable Protein (TVP): Used as a meat substitute, TVP is made from soy flour and is extremely high in protein. It's also inexpensive and great for plant-based eating on a budget. It comes in little flakes or chunks and can be found in the bulk section of health food stores or online. My favorite use for TVP is in chili because the texture is perfect for replacing ground beef and it simply soaks up all the flavors—meat eaters don't even notice the difference!

Tofu: Made from soybeans, water and a coagulant, aka curdling agent, tofu is high in protein and calcium. Tofu has a neutral flavor and can soak up any flavors added to it, making it versatile in recipes. Pressing it before marinating it is especially important so that flavor can take the place of excess water within the tofu. Tofu comes in a variety of textures, from extra-firm (good for baking and sautéing) to silken (great for blending into sauces, dips, smoothies and puddings).

ACKNOWLEDGMENTS

Today is all about living each moment with gratitude and the will to be our best selves—This is the gateway to our own happiness and to bringing joy and inspiration to others.

—Ella Magers

I am grateful to the countless people throughout my life who have supported my growth as an individual since the day I was born. My mom and dad built the foundation of empowering love that allowed me to use my strong-willed spirit to stand up for what I believed in from a very early age. There are no words to describe the depth of my gratitude and love for them. I couldn't feel more fortunate for having such amazing friends and family who played a role, both directly and indirectly, in the creation of this book. I can always count on Diana, Anne and Silvia, girlfriends who may as well be sisters, to have my back. Thank you to Sheryn, a friend and outstanding vegan chef who I've learned so much from over the years. Thanks to my friend and talented artist Julia Veli, for being a mom to Shye, my rescue Chihuahua who owns my heart. I want to thank Rob for having incredible confidence in me and love for me. Also, a big thank you to Johnny for believing in me, Brian for your encouragement, Ronni for your help and support, my sister Anna, who is incredibly beautiful from the inside out, and my amazing grandmother Mimi, who was chopping vegetables and testing recipes for me at 94 years old!

Last but certainly not least, I want to thank Will and the entire Page Street Publishing team for recognizing my passion and authenticity, and believing in me enough to bring this book into being.

CREDITS

Photographer: Michael Reh (www.michaelreh.com)

Cover: Anthony Golston (www.anthonygolston.com)

Wardrobe: Julia Veli (orange painted shirt over dark blue dress in photo with apple)

Mauricio Esquenazi, Peixoto Swim & Resort Wear (red bathing suit)

Stylists: Julia Veli, Stehanie Maia

ABOUT THE AUTHOR

ELLA'S greatest passion is to share with people her knowledge and experiences, past and present, that have helped her attain a lifestyle that is not only healthy and compassionate, but also sexy and exhilarating.

Ella's journey started in the third grade when she connected her love of animals to the food on her plate and decided never to eat meat again. Her deep sense of compassion for all living creatures soon led her to transition to a fully vegan lifestyle.

Ella's focus on fitness began at a young age as she participated in a variety of sports: swimming, gymnastics, dance and volleyball. After college, Ella jumped right into her career in the fitness and wellness industry, and opportunity brought her from her beautiful home state of North Carolina to hot, sexy Miami Beach. There, she was able to combine her passions with a career helping people become fit and healthy through exercise and nutrition.

Ella has been a fitness and wellness professional for 12+ years, with her certifications in Personal Training from the National Academy of Sports Medicine and Wellness Coaching from the University of Miami. She specializes in functional, bodyweight and cross-training, as well as Muay Thai kickboxing. She obtained her Masters Degree in Social Work to gain additional skills in counseling clients as they work through hardships, gain success and strive for a happy, healthy life.

As a fitness competitor, Ella won the 2007 FAME Fitness World Championship in the bikini category, as well as taking second in the fitness and fitness model categories. She has been featured as a fitness expert in the media, including appearances on "CBS Health News Reports" and in publications such as *Prevention*, *Ms. Fitness* and *Modern Bride* magazines.

Ella created her brand, Sexy Fit Vegan®™, and website, SexyFitVegan.com, in order to educate, motivate, and inspire people to transition to a healthy vegan lifestyle. Ella also consults for companies, helping in the development and improvement of vegan and fitness-related projects. In 2013, she consulted for DeliverLean, South Florida's fastest growing meal preparation and delivery service, working closely with the chefs to create a "Sexy Fit Vegan Approved" meal plan.

In September 2013, Ella was named Personal Trainer of the Month on the world's most popular fitness and body building website, BodyBuilding.com. In 2014, she was honored to be named as part of *Shape* magazine's "50 Hottest Trainers in America." Ella has also been featured on numerous websites such as HauteLiving.com, TheHealthSite.com, RealTalkRealWomen.com and LifeOfAFighter.com.

In addition to *The Six Weeks to Sexy Abs Meal Plan*, Ella has authored several ebooks featured on SexyFitVegan.com. She enjoys conducting vegan wellness workshops, most recently traveling to Macao, China, for Sheraton's Fitness Connection Month. Ella is currently working toward her doctorate in Holistic Sports Nutrition and plans to continue on her path toward fulfilling the Sexy Fit Vegan® mission: To empower people with the tools they need to make conscious choices and live a life they love.

INDEX